D1149638

PORTRAIT OF
A MASTER
CRAFTSMAN

JIM HANDYSIDE

AMBASSADOR PRODUCTIONS LTD.
Providence House
16 Hillview Avenue
Belfast BT5 6JR

Copyright © 1987 by Jim Handyside

First Published 1987

All rights reserved. No part of this publication may be reproduced, stored in a retrieval system, or transmitted , in any form or by any means, electronic, mechanical, photocopying, recording or otherwise, without the prior permission in writing, of the publisher.

ISBN 0 907927 18 1

Printed in Northern Ireland by
Ambassador Productions

ACKNOWLEDGEMENTS

To my daughter, Mrs. J. Primrose, M.A.Hons., Dip.Ed. for proof-reading, corrections and helpful suggestions.

To Mrs. Violet McKeown for personal papers belonging to her husband and invaluable information.

To: S. M. Houghton M. A. Abingdon, England.
    John Blewer, Esq., Owensboro, Kentucky, U.S.A.
    Hector Gillies, Esq., Applecross, Wester Ross, Scotland.
and many Christian friends for assistance and encouragement.

Raymond McKeown

CONTENTS

INTRODUCTION

Raymond McKeown, nurtured in the city whose motto once read, "Let Glasgow flourish by the preaching of the Word and the praising of His Name," did more than the majority of his fellow citizens to obey that injunction. One of the primary qualities in a life, if the bestowal of the title "great" be properly granted, must be humility. It was this very characteristic which has denied a larger public the privilege of knowing much about this unsung hero of the Cross.

Events unfolded in this book should go some way to rectifying this ommission, and should set forth for the Christian populace particularly, an historical record of apostolic labours in a twentieth century setting. To say that Raymond McKeown ranked with the truly great men in Scotland's religious history is not an exaggeration. An incisive intellect, logical mind of sharp theological perception, and a highly developed native wit, couple these with the inherent ability of knowing exactly what made his fellow working class Clydesiders tick, and you come close to the genius of the man!

To lionise Raymond would be an offence to his memory and would be contrary to his own practical and stated belief, "that in all things Christ might have the pre-eminence." In saluting the servant, we salute the Master who made him what he was.

PROLOGUE

The emergence of an outstanding and unique talent in Christian circles is not common but is always exciting. For that talent to be maintained and developed over many years is a source of real encouragement and benefit to the Christian community at large. The prime motivating factor in the writing of this book was to set before a wider public, a life with a multiplicity of gifts and graces, that cried out to be recorded in a day when there is a scarcity of giants in the land.

Let there be no confusion when we assert that the life and works of Raymond McKeown rank with the great men of the past. Whilst conceding the impossibility or even the advisability of making direct comparions with previous men of God, yet some facts are worthy of consideration when making a case for the publication of this biography.

Scotland, with a population of a few millions, has, nevertheless, produced per head, probably more theologians, missionaries, ministers of integrity and power, than any other nation in the world. John Knox heads a glorious list, his son-in-law John Welch was a man of unusual power and gifts, as were Robert Murray McCheyne, William Burns, Robert Bruce, Thomas Chalmers, the Erskine brothers and Thomas Boston. The covenanting stock included Cargill, Renwick, Cameron, the Guthries and Rutherford. Later came the Bonars and such men as "Rabbi" John Duncan and James Kennedy of Dingwall.

What characterised those men? They were holy, dedicated, knowledgeable, self-less and made their mark upon their generation. They were pillars of the Reformed faith and many have lamented their passing. Sadly, this lament has sometimes obscured the possibility that a sovereign God could still raise up such men in the present day. The qualities that sometimes appear necessary today, if a man is to be "recorded for posterity," even with such attributes as here delineated, is that he must have been dead for many, many years.

Raymond McKeown was a holy man of God, and few who knew him personally could imagine how any of the men on the foregoing list might have been much holier. He was a single minded dedicated outstanding servant of God. While it is true that many of the outstanding men listed could have excelled him in various areas, those who knew and observed Raymond's total commitment, would find it hard to imagine many demonstrating more practical Christianity than he did. Knox was outstanding in the impact he made upon his native land, as Father of the Scottish nation and founder of the Scottish church. The thousands who were challenged through the ministry of Raymond McKeown, make it difficult to conceive that any of the others did more in their times to exercise a greater influence on their generation.

The humility and holiness of life could not have been more ably manifested by the godly McCheyne. The highly developed theological grasp was not dwarfed by the abilities of Boston or the Erskines. The consuming love and missionary zeal for the souls of men would have found the approval of William Burns, and one might have to go back to the days of Wesley and Whitefield in the open air evangelistic field, to find a parallel.

The Calvinists do not have so many "jewels in their crown" in the twentieth century, especially in the evangelistic realm, as to cause them to be indifferent to Raymond McKeown, the "master craftsman" of fiery, primitive biblical evangelism

Chapter 1

Early Years and Conversion

Belfast in 1925 simmered under the imposition of partition. This "solution" to the complex age-old problem of Ulster was a compromise. Because of its instinctive thinking of Ireland as a single and political whole, Irish Nationalism certainly did not view partition as the answer. Paradoxically, the establishment of Home Rule in Ulster was no un-qualified victory for Ulster Unionists either, for ironically, they had fought to be governed from Westminister as was the rest of the United Kingdom.

This was the existing background in 1925 when Joseph and Margaret McKeown welcomed their third child — Raymond — into the world. Joseph, a Sergeant in the Royal Ulster Constabulary and a staunch Presbyterian, lived in the Protestant enclave of the Antrim Road in Belfast. Thus, Eric, Eileen and Raymond McKeown began life in a solid, respectable working class environment in Northern Ireland. Ruth, the youngest of the family, was born in Glasgow.

Social life in Ulster revolved much around the churches and associated organisations. For the Protestant community, the maintaining of their culture and way of life was paramount. The Orange Order was a powerful organ integrated into the social and political life of Ulster. July 12th celebrations commemerated the Battle of the Boyne where Irish Protestantism sided with William of Orange in his successful attempt to wrest the English throne from Catholic James II.

The flamboyant Orange marches, divided into numerous Lodges, were a very cohesive force. The colour, noise, excitement and drama of an Orange Walk is unforgettable — the foot tapping rhythmic urge of the flute and accordion band, the compelling thud of the giant Lambeg drums, the mace throwing, the evocative swaying and rolling, stimulated by the cheers of the gathered thousands, and surely patriotic fervour and un-dying allegiance to the Protestant cause is assured. Since around 1830, Ulster has been a stronghold of fundamental evangelicalism, accepting the Bible as the literal Word of God. This evangelicalism was strongly impregnated with Presbyterianism which practised and propagated the old Reformation principles of the justified soul being granted free access into the direct presence of its God and Saviour. The Roman Catholic Baltimore Catechism states: "Confession is the telling of our sins to an authorised priest for the purpose of obtaining forgiveness." Couple this heresy to the view that Popery is a vigorous and sinister political system, with the Jesuits acknowledging none their master in political intrigue. These factors were all the ingredients necessary for polarisation in the explosive cauldron of ungovernable Ulster.

Joseph McKeown, having served in the Army and latterly the R.U.C., felt trapped, as did many of his fellow countrymen, by the bleak ineptitude of the British Government's repeated failure to deal with the problems of the turbulent Province. Torn with a dilemma of National identity; on the one hand proud of their Irish heritage, but on the other, British in their strenuous efforts to thwart the overall Roman Catholic majority's insistence on a united Ireland.

"The Troubles," as the Anglo-Irish war was designated, commenced in 1919 and the Republican forces, latterly known as the I.R.A., waged escalating guerilla warfare against the British. Although 1921 saw the installation of the new Regional Government of Northern Ireland, the active antagonism of the Nationalists saw them still pledging open allegiance to Dail Eirean in the South. All this and increasing I.R.A. violence was beginning to weigh heavily upon men like Joseph McKeown. The final straw in motivating his decision to leave his native shore came when his wife was shot at by those who had no love for an ex-army man and serving R.U.C. officer.

Kirkintilloch was a small country town overlooking the Campsie Hills a few miles north-east of Glasgow. It was here that the McKeown family first settled after leaving Ulster. The story of Raymond McKeown's life and ministry might have been vastly different if a certain course of events had run their course. Joseph McKeown had made application to the Canadian Royal Mounted Police and, upon acceptance, was ready to go to Winnipeg. However, his wife finally drew back and could not go through with the prospect of emigrating. So, in a short space of time the family moved to the

Gorbals area of Glasgow. Oatlands Primary School received the McKeown children for their early education. Joseph secured a job in the Glasgow Corporation and the family settled into life in Scotland, socially and religiously, much as they had done in Belfast. The early years in the Gorbals area made their imprint on Raymond's life and thinking. His identification with the "cloth cap" Glasgow working man image, remained with him all his life, though somewhat refined by the passing of time. The West of Scotland has long been a Socialist stronghold and his seeds of interest in the class war, were nurtured from early school days in an environmental climate admirably suited to their fruitful germination.

The McKeown family had to maintain the Protestant tradition deeply etched in the soul of the Ulsterman! Joseph McKeown soon became Secretary of the Hutchesontown Prize Flute Band and the stalwart Orangeman and proud Drum Major had already enlisted his sons within the ranks of the flutes and drums. When he was about thirteen, Raymond moved with his family to Househillwood which was a few miles west of the Gorbals.

Schooldays for the McKeown family took place during the great Depression. The Thirties were a black time for employment in Clydeside and poorer families struggled to make ends meet. Down at the shipyards where Raymond was destined to engage in some of his finest ministry, men gathered morning by morning and literally ran in droves after the Bowler hatted shipyard foremen begging for jobs. They had to swallow their pride and humiliate themselves for the possibility of earning a little to maintain their families.

Thirteen-year-old Raymond McKeown progressed to Shawlands Academy to complete his educational process. Thoughts of his schooldays at this establishment never conjured up happy memories for him. There were a minority of children from the poorer working class districts around Shawlands, who, by virtue of their academic prowess, were admitted into the more rarefied halls of learning. Raymond was one of these, but they were social outcasts, never really accepted or integrated into the upper echelons of society, who predominated at Shawlands Academy in those days. These were formative times in the boy's character building and he could never feel at home in such a class conscious atmosphere. A short time before his death, on a visit to Glasgow, Raymond and Violet passed by the old Academy and he remarked "Oh!, I will always remember that place, I was never accepted in it."

11

The Tent Hall in Glasgow which came into being after the visit of D. L. Moody at the beginning of the century, began to be frequented by the McKeown family on a regular basis. Margaret McKeown had come to a saving knowledge of Christ, and proved a good influence in shepherding the whole family along to the evangelistic services. This strategy paid off handsomely, because before long Joseph, Eileen and Ruth had joined Margaret McKeown in a personal salvation experience. Eric McKeown had gone off to the R.A.F. and only Raymond remained unconverted.

Father, mother and daughters now began to make the rebel a consistent objective of their prayers. The diversity of gifts latent in Raymond's personality began to emerge in his teenage years. The parents recognised that an excellent singing voice was amongst these gifts. One of Glasgow's finest singing teachers, who had also enrolled another promising young singer called Kenneth McKellar, found the young McKeown an apt and promising pupil. At this time Raymond had a burning desire to perform on the light operatic stage and with the zeal that characterised so many of his later ambitions, this goal seemed eminently possible.

Attendance at the old Tent hall now began to diminish as Raymond's other interests propelled him inevitably away from religious exercise. A keen footballer, he proceeded to demonstrate that in the sporting realm also he had some potential, and eventually he was playing for Pollok Juniors which was only a step away from Senior Professional football. The ambivalence produced by these conflicting interests, showed in his decreasing visits to the Tent Hall. The family were often shocked to the core of their orthodox evangelical souls when Raymond signalled any disagreement with what was declared from the platform by rising and walking out!

Argyle Street in Glasgow and its immediate precincts, were the location of all kinds of open air meetings, especially at the weekends. Every shade of political opinion was aired with varying degrees of accuracy and skill, and likewise little "holy huddles" with sombre men in dark suits and noticeably joyless exteriors, would intone regarding judgment to come. Raymond was particularly arrested by an anarchist called Eddie. Some sympathy for his line of thought did develop, but the gathering of information was also helpful in the amassing of facts that would later be used in deadly fashion in the noble art of heckling of which Raymond became a master.

Singing, football, amateur dramatics, political aspirations, would there be no end to the multi-faceted interests and abilities of a working class Irish youth from a God-fearing humble Unionist/Orange background? There were no "amateur dramatics" the night Raymond's mother uncovered a hidden copy of Darwin's the "Origin of Species" in his room. That was the ultimate blasphemy and the poor woman was overcome with grief and weeping. That her beloved son should have sunk to such ignominy was a cruel blow.

Foot and Ball's Handbook was the "bible" of the Secular Society. It purported to list every discrepancy in the Bible and was faithfully carried by Raymond everywhere he went. Whether Paine, Ingersoll, Darwin or Huxley, the teen-age rebel had a voracious appetite for the works of the atheist or agnostic writers, and was confidently if respectfully, expounding their views to the godly family in Househillwood.

The climax to the disputing and arguments, often culled from the "Free Thinker" paper, was that Joseph McKeown in a moment of sheer frustration at his son's attitude and assertions, turned on him and said, "If you are so convinced of these great truths and arguments, why don't you get yourself a soapbox and go tell the world about them?" This unfortunately did not have the intended effect upon his son that Joseph had anticipated, because that is just exactly what Raymond did!

Brunswick Street, adjacent to Argyle Street in Glasgow, was the mecca of the political agitators and young McKeown set up his box and waded in with the best of them. Argyle Street in the early forties, throbbed with life on Saturday nights as late shoppers thronged Woolworths, Marks and Spencers and Lewis's stores. The old trams clanged amidst the milling crowds. The Red one for Auchenshuggle, the Blue one for Parkhead, the Green for Airdrie, part and parcel all of them of the seemingly unchanging Glasgow scene. And so also were the agitators, the cranks, the zealots who competed with the Saturday evening noise and hustle to draw their own particular audience.

A benign Deity, surveying the scene where an earnest young man tilted his lance in quixotic abandon against the divine precepts, knew, what a sorrowing and anxious mother would have given much to know right then. The heart of Raymond McKeown was soon to find a new un-dying allegiance. Brunswick Street would hear from the rebel again, even as Jerusalem heard from Saul of Tarsus, and both would repudiate with great vehemence that which they formerly and most strenuously asserted. It was not just the religious aspect that created tension in the McKeown household, but the political also. The Protestant inhabitants of the Six Counties which constituted Northern Ireland, embraced Ulster Unionism for pragmatic reasons of necessity, and not primarily because they were avowed Conservatives. The alternative of Irish Nationalism, particularly as represented by Sinn Fein (Ourselves), was unthinkable. Such habits and convictions die hard, so Raymond's anarchist views of this period were a sad provocation and continual irritation to the whole family.

There is tremendous encouragement here for all Christians who have prayed for loved ones and found the task discouraging, and to all natural appearances hopeless. Preceding Raymond's conversion to Christ, the outlook seemed remarkably bleak and discouraging. On many evenings the family would be at prayer when he would come in late from his various ventures, tip-toeing past them as he made his way to bed. Who could seem a more unlikely candidate for God's salvation than a rebellious anarchist propagating his atheistic views even amongst his own devoted Christian family. But the "Spirit of the Lord is not straitened!"

Raymond was allowed to absent himself from all the services in the Tent Hall except the Sunday afternoon Bible class conducted by R. C. Brown. Converted through the ministry of D. L. Moody, Brown had the deserved reputation of a very godly man, and a well-loved Bible teacher. Although Raymond and some other youths, probably also under some compulsion to be there, were often inattentive, and fooled about, yet God was preparing some hearts for the coming of the Holy Spirit in saving power.

Jock Troup, already a legend in his own time, was Superintendent of the Tent Hall, which, under successive godly Superintendents, was one of the great evangelistic centres of the world. First, as assistant to P. T. McRostie in 1932 and then from the following year until 1945, Jock Troup directed activities in the great Saltmarket Mission called the Tent Hall. Open air meetings at Glasgow Cross attracted hundreds of people and amongst the crowd on one occasion was Raymond the anarchist. Moved by the things he heard, he later made his way to the evening service, and, sitting in the balcony, could survey his two sisters in the choir, and his parents in their regular place down below. When Troup in his blunt and simple presentation of the Gospel, appealed for those to make it known who would trust Christ, the rebel, the anarchist, the actor, the singer, the sportsman, the estranged soul who could never quite subdue the inward conviction that perhaps his godly family were right after all, made his repentant way to reconciliation. Leaving the auditorium, he retired to a side room with one of the workers, himself a converted alcoholic, and found Christ as Lord and Saviour at seventeen years of age.

Ruth vividly remembers the occasion. "I cannot describe the feeling. I watched him rise and go to seek counsel. It was like a dream, I was stunned." That night Raymond came home and announced that he had given his life to Christ. The McKeown family knew then in a deeper way that there was a God in heaven who heard and answered prayer!

The Apostle Paul had a dramatic "Damascus Road" experience which every Christian has not necessarily known. Raymond did, however, have a "Damascus Road" experience, total, radical, absolute, exceeding anything known in the rabid, fervent fanaticism of the political extremes hitherto embraced. Even his being a Conscientious Objector paled when compared to this event, likewise the philosophy which envisioned a bright new world through extreme political expediency. He had got a dose of good old time religion and the change was immediate, he was a new creation. The old things not only passed away, but rather seemed instantly annihilated. He was born again and the turn-about was somewhat awesome in its initial transformation.

Literally overnight, the amateur dramatics, light opera aspirations, the sporting interests, but, above all, the extreme political affiliations, dissolved. His family could hardly believe the miraculous change. Some of the "old worthies" who abounded in the Tent Hall then, took Raymond under their wing and his singing was utilised in visitations to other Mission Halls, as was his testimony in the back court open air work, for which the Tent was renowned. Raymond was serving his apprenticeship, not only as a joiner, but in the hard reality of Christian service as a young worker in the Tent Hall. This situation continued for about two years until he had finished his apprenticeship as a joiner, and one week after receiving his "lines" as a fully accredited tradesman, he declared his intention of serving God in some full-time capacity.

15

Chapter 2

Marriage and Early Labours

Nineteen-Forty-Two dawned with the nation grimly struggling for survival in a global war of attrition. Being a Conscientious Objector, though not yet a Christian, Raymond had his apprenticeship interrupted to be given a "reserved occupation." These were jobs allocated to those engaged in work of national importance such as munitions, shipbuilding and the like, and to be thus employed exempted the worker from military service. Conscientious Objectors were also directed into such occupations.

Exemption from military service, however, was no absolute guarantee of security or isolation from the horrific reality of a World War. In 1941 Clydeside, particularly the shipyard town of Clydebank, suffered horrendous damage through the "Blitz," and, in two nights, the greater part of the town was destroyed or damaged. Paradoxically though, prime targets such as John Brown's shipyard and the Singer sewing machine factory, then engaged in munitions work were practically unscathed.

Raymond went to work with J. and R. Wilson, Shipping Store merchants in Oswald Street, Glasgow, in a "reserved occupation." Wilson's supplied troopships with their stores and provisions and therefore were engaged in work vital to the war effort. Although not on the front line, Raymond like the rest of the Clydeside civilian population, often heard the air-raid siren wail out its doleful warning of approaching enemy aircraft bent on the destruction of the numerous shipyards and factories scattered around Clydeside.

Charlie Wylie, a staunch Brethren believer, also worked in Wilson's and lost no time in presenting the Gospel to the latest addition to the workforce. Charlie was initially unaware that the McKeown family were making Raymond a target of prayer and Providence was surely outworking God's redemptive plan with the final pieces of the divine jigsaw irrevocably poised to fall into place.

After a year or so, Raymond was able to leave Wilson's and resume

16

his apprenticeship as a joiner. When he was converted he quickly decided that one of the first people who should hear the good news was his old workmate Charlie Wylie. Charlie was overjoyed at this and immediately decided to take the new convert under his wing by inviting him to his home in Partick on a regular basis The Wylie's had a young daughter called Violet, and she recalls these times in her own words. "He came to us regularly every Wednesday night, and I can always remember that as soon as the supper dishes were cleared away Raymond and my father would sit around the table and talk." Charlie did most of the talking. Raymond was often to describe these times as akin to when the Apostle Paul sat at the feet of Gamaliel and was instructed concerning the law of God. Charlie was well versed in the Scriptures and the glorious doctrines of the faith were unfolded to Raymond in the weekly evening get-togethers. The seed sown was to germinate later in Raymond as he became a convinced and immovable believer in the Doctrines of Grace, commonly called Calvinism.

Visitations to the Wylie home continued for about three years and Raymond became increasingly interested in the fact that Violet had certain musical abilities. This common interest and their love of Christ drew them closer and eventually, near the end of this period, they went out together. Raymond's determination to fulfil his calling into full-time service for God led him to Salem Bible College in Gillingham. After a short time there he was accepted as an assistant at the Glyn Vivian Miners Mission in Deal, Kent, and he laboured there till his interview for the Open Air Mission in 1949.

The interview for the Open Air Mission and the prospect of at last fulfilling the burning ambition to serve God in this capacity prompted Raymond to write some verses to Violet which mirror his emotion at the time. He entitled the poem "Consecration."

In the glad morning of my day my life I give.
Make me to walk the narrow way,
Teach me in all I do and say, for Thee to live.
Gracious Redeemer, give the sight that seeth Thee,
That Thou, who art the Life, the Light,
Taking away my sinful night, might shine through me.

Dear Lord and Master of my life, thy love impart,
Free me from earthly war and sinful strife,
Live out Thy risen glorious life within my heart.
Take then this offering of mine to be thine own.

All my possessions I resign,
Purge, purify and make them thine and thine alone.

Raymond and Violet courted for seven years before they were finally married in the old Grove Street Institute in Glasgow. Prior to the marriage in December, 1953, they had discussed the priority of God in their relationship, especially in the area of time allocation. Raymond with a remarkable degree of perception and insight for a young man, realised by observation, the stumbling block that many Christian wives erected by their insistence upon primacy in their husbands' affections and time. Knowing that this sometimes gravely inhibited the effectiveness of a man's ministry, it is to the credit of the young couple that they resolved to avoid this pitfall by God's grace. It was therefore, in a measure due to Violet's submission to the terms of their youthful covenant that Raymond was able to engage in such a demanding ministry.

Raymond and Violet made their first home in Coatbridge a few miles from Glasgow and attended the large Coatdyke Brethern Assembly near by. With Raymond being in the Open Air Mission and regularly away from home, the actual location of a home was not critically important. The single apartment just happened to become available in Coatbridge and the princely sum of £50 was raised for its purchase! From Coatbridge the couple then moved to a two apartment home in Dumbarton Road, Partick, and they were to reside in Glasgow for many years. At this time they attended Abingdon Hall, Partick and thus Raymond continued his association with Brethren Assemblies which began soon after his conversion. Following this they worshipped in Greenview Hall in the South side of the city. It was necessary that the workers in the Tent Hall should have a church to attend, as the Tent Hall did not function in this capacity, having no Sunday morning worship service, for example.

Raymond, as a full-time preacher with the Open Air Mission, was soon enlisted into the open air work of Abingdon Hall when he was available. All went well for a time, until when conducting a service one Sunday evening, at Merkland Street, he called upon a young lady, a missionary home on furlough, to testify of God's saving grace at the open air meeting. This was not well received by certain sections of the Assembly, although others, notably younger members, had no objections. Raymond, however, always fearful of causing strife or schism, foresaw the possibility of division in the future over such matters and felt (in the cause of unity), he would be better to leave

18

in an unobtrusive manner. Raymond's constant forays with the Open Air Mission did not make church membership a critical issue for the young couple, so Violet joined herself to a little Mission Hall adjacent to the home, whose services were conducted by a doyen of evangelism at that time, one, "Daddy Hart!" The Gospel exploits of "Daddy" which included founding a Mission in North India, would require a separate volume.

Raymond's political persuasions were rooted in Socialism. That larger than life portrayal of the "cloth cap" Glasgow working man, which in humorous moments he loved to caricature, was close to his heart. The tremendous empathy which was manifested when he held sway over the crowds in the open air meetings, was born of a genuine, proud identification with the working class and was something they instinctively recognised.

When the fires of extreme Left Wing Socialism were cooled by conversion to Christ, Raymond still retained the Socialism of James Keir Hardie, founder and father figure of the British Labour Party. Hardie was a coal miner who had been greatly influenced by the works of Robert Burns, Scotland's national poet, and Thomas Carlyle, who was a Pacifist. The tales of the Scottish Covenanters were precious to him as Hardie had become a Christian around 1878 at 22 years of age. He was eventually elected to Parliament as member for Merthyr Tydfil for the Independent Labour Party, which he represented for the remainder of his active life. Raymond treasured a poem of Hardie's, a verse of which reads as follows:

> May the loving arms o' Jesus draw us
> near Him as He whispers,
> A hope o' life for ever,
> Free frae worldly care and strife,
> May we fa' asleep commitin',
> Oor souls into His keepin',
> Till we wauken i' the mornin',
> Born tae everlastin' life.

Keir Hardie was seen as Christian, Crusader, Champion of the down-trodden, fiery orator and radical politician, pleading the cause of the dispossessed. This was all the Socialism which Raymond embraced, and in Hardie he found an amalgam of Christianity and political philosophy which appealed to his own thinking. Raymond could say that "during my tenure as a shop steward in Clydeside I found a name held in high esteem in the Trade Union movement was that of James Keir Hardie." Raymond could continue, "What

19

was the secret of the burning compassion and concern of Keir Hardie? — simply that he knew Christ as his Saviour, and the love of Christ shed abroad in his heart. This engendered a desire to see the oppressed helped and comforted.' Although staunch in his Socialist views, Raymond was no programmed political pundit with blind allegiance to a party dogma. On the contrary, he often manifested as something of a shaft of conscience to the Labour and Trade Union movement, as he reminded them of principles which were supposed to be part of their tradition and belief. This is ably demonstrated in a letter written to a local newspaper during an anti-pornography campaign in Glasgow.

"Dear Sir,
Congratulations on your stand against the proposed Partick Porn Shop.

Writing as a former Clydeside shop steward, I would fully expect the Labour Party and all other political organisations which professedly oppose exploitation for financial gain to come out into the open and unequivocally declare themselves against this sordid trade in human degradation for profit.

If the usually articulate Left Wing keeps quiet on this issue a lot of working men like myself will have good reason to doubt their integrity."

"The Spirit of the Lord is upon me, because He hath anointed me to preach the Gospel to the poor; He hath sent me to heal the broken-hearted, to preach deliverance to the captives, and recovering of sight to the blind, to set at liberty them that are bruised." This commission and qualification of the Saviour in Luke's Gospel was the driving force in His servant Raymond McKeown.

That the Gospel was primarily for the poor Raymond had no doubt, but political beliefs did not overtly intrude into his declaration of the Evangel. It might have to be conceded that the down-and-out, the under-privileged, and the working class generally, received the main thrust of his ministry. Doubtless this was an admirable objective, although a minor criticism sometimes expressed was that some of the other classes of society felt that a touch of deification of the proletariat inhibited the possibility of closer fellowship. Whilst there may have been slight justification in this viewpoint, nevertheless it has to be recorded that Raymond also displayed considerable interest in the student and professional classes, and the little home "up a close" in Partick had a considerable cross-section of these in the continual stream of visitors who esteemed a visit to the

McKeown home and the opportunity of a chat with Raymond to be of inestimable spiritual value.

Some clue to the magnetism which Raymond exuded to all sectors of the Christian populace in search of help, instruction, or guidance might have been gleaned by the observant in their every day contact with him. Raymond was seldom encountered without some volume protruding from his working overalls! He had an amazing capacity for secreting all manner of theological tomes on his person, and this habit of avid, almost voracious devouring of Christian literature, combined with an exceedingly retentive memory system, made him much sought-after when advice was required. They came from all sections of evangelical society and few indeed felt that the "pilgrimage to Partick" was an unprofitable exercise.

Reading has become something of a lost art to modern day busy evangelicals, but Raymond did much to combat this failure by instilling interest in reading by example. Both immature and experienced believers were motivated to an intake of biblical knowledge and to draw upon and apply such for the practicalities of every day Christian living.

Raymond's preaching was interesting, imaginative, and instructive and this was due in no small measure not only to Scriptural knowledge but to his vast interest in literature of all kinds. Many evangelical pulpits lack this ingredient and the ministry is often boring and un-imaginative, some of the malaise can surely be traced to an inability or lack of desire to absorb the writings that God has seen fit to bless through outstanding men appointed by Him to be mentors of the church. There can be no doubt that this encouraging of the reading habit was a vital and profitable peripheral ministry which Raymond often unconsciously manifested.

Spurgeon, whom Raymond greatly admired and continually read, has surely been responsible through his writing for the inspiring of thousands in the Christian ministry, missionary labour or zealous evangelisation by ordinary church members. From his political background, Raymond was well acquaint with the emphasis the Communist particularly, but all political parties, put upon the printed word, and its ability to excite men to change and inspire to courses of action. In this respect Raymond did much service to the gospel by impressing many with the benefits of reading and absorbing Christian literature. Though bereft of the opportunity of a university education, Raymond nevertheless diligently applied himself to a systematic study of the Word of God and all things theological which made him inferior to few in his understanding of doctrinal truth. To argue or debate with Raymond was to come against a clinically logical mind, which soon reduced an argument to its essential components, and set them in order of priority and relevance. Those in debate often felt that they had been engaged in a verbal game of chess with a Grand Master and had suddenly arrived at checkmate. Yet it had all been done so graciously and in such a friendly spirit that it was almost a pleasure to be relieved of one's weapons of polemic and be more perfectly instructed! An excellent example of Raymond in full flight on the question of evolution is related here from the "Free Thinker," April, 1956.

Dear Sir,

The more rational of your readers will have noticed in Mr. Cutner's answer to my letter that he has sought to obscure the issue of the Haeckel falsifications, by the questionable method of introducing such red herrings as Billy Graham, Christian Scientists, and Jehovah's Witnesses. For good measure, there is a hilarious claim that all the Germans except scientists like Haeckel, were Christians. This is solemnly claimed with the assurance of one who has doubtlessly personally interviewed the whole eighty million of them!

And if Brass's evidence is to be discounted because someone with an axe to grind claimed that he was a liar, your readers will know how to treat Mr. Cutner's evidence.

Mr. Cutner would have us believe that the only falsification in scientific diagrams was that made by the transfer from the scientist's mind to the drawing board of the artist. But this is, to say the least of it, misleading.

Readers with long memories will remember the two-page illustration in one of the London illustrated magazines, of a full grown male and his spouse in natural surroundings, and dignified by the appelation "Hesperopithecus." There was a full description of this happy pair by a "professor" from one of our "great universities." The model for this monument of evolutionary genius was — one tooth — discovered in 1922. The tooth was later found to belong to a pig. But the artist no doubt had trouble with one or two "inaccuracies" which "were bound to occur."

A dog's dinner of bones was "reconstructed" by "artists" no doubt with a few inescapable "inaccuracies" and became Piltdown man, that answer to the prayer of Keith, from a "great university." The whole thing, as every music hall comedian knows, was a great joke. And so the wreck of the "Hesperopithecus" and the "bones of contention" from Piltdown man, are conveniently forgotten and poor artists have to bear the brunt of the blame.

In the light of this, I think biologists who are teaching in "religious" and "theological" colleges have more sense than Mr. Cutner would credit them with. After all, if "biology" professors from "great universities" cannot distinguish between pigs' teeth and fully-grown males, one can't blame the stick-in-the-mud religionist for staying where he is.

If Mr. Cutner would read R. E. D. Clark's book — which I trust he will — he would find out that Darwin lived in mortal terror of ever being convinced that his "hypothesis" was wrong since, from his youth, he had been trying to escape from the possibility of there being a God who would hold men responsible. So Mr. Cutner's argument works both ways. If the theory (Mr. Cutner has admitted that there is no mathematical demonstration) of evolution be proved correct, then I am of all men, most miserable; if Mr. Cutner be wrong, what then? Or is the good man infallible?

R. McKeown

This is only one example of numerous letters which Raymond wrote to all kinds of magazines and periodicals on a vast range of topics related to a defence of the Christian position.

In the Fifties, especially in the numerous lanes off Renfield Street and Argyle Street in Glasgow, Raymond could be found on most Saturday afternoons rummaging through the contents of the two wheelbarrows stacked with a miscellany of literature old and new. Many a "pearl" could be un-earthed by the discerning seeker and Raymond was unexcelled in that capability. One could place an "order" for some obscure or unobtainable Christian volume and inevitably Raymond, with the persistence of a bloodhound, would eventually un-earth the volume from his continual forays. "The Scots Worthies" or "Cloud of Witnesses," those out of print classics of the Scottish Covenanters, were regularly acquired by Raymond for grateful applicants from the most unlikely sources. For a few shillings, many a saint appropriated a priceless volume, and more often than not, received it as a gift from one who seemed to consider the successful tracking down of an elusive volume to be ample reward for the labour involved.

It was a confession of Raymond's that after his usually arduous labours at various open air meetings and church programmes, that he often loved to relax before dropping off for a well earned night's rest, with a good old-fashioned Western full of gun smoke and lead slinging! Even some of the children's books such as "Biggles" adventures were often filched surreptiously! The apparent trivia of such a pursuit nevertheless provided the necessary winding-down process that engaging in spiritual warfare demanded. Raymond as ever, had his own homespun remedies for the stress and strain of wholehearted endeavour to extend the Kingdom of God.

Chapter 3

The Open Air Mission

Bustling, noisy, crowded, colourful Epsom Downs horse racing track on Derby Day, 1950. Hardly seems the most likely venue for the birth of a spiritual partnership. Willie Docherty, a douce, dogged Scots evangelist with the Open Air Mission, first met his prospective new partner, a budding preacher called Raymond McKeown midst the bookies and punters. The pair presented something of a contrast. Willie, big, raw-boned, dependable, with a background of the Plymouth Brethren to keep his feet firmly rooted on terra firma; Raymond on the other hand, a thin, sharp-witted, young man, now in his mid-twenties, impatient to fulfil the burning conviction of God's call to the open air ministry. An unlikely combination perhaps, but one that was to prove most effective in the five years of unified labour that lay ahead.

Willie soon recognised the unusual gifts of his co-worker and wisely shaped the partnership to accommodate these. Kinghorn, in Fife, was the first place where the new pair were scheduled to work together. The art of gathering a crowd is an absolutely essential part of the open air preacher's armoury. Raymond's talent was as yet un-developed in this area, and Willie, as senior partner, took upon himself the skilful ministry of "baiting the hook." Successful meetings in Kinghorn ratified the partnership officially and off to Birmingham went the two evangelists, to collect a new van specially equipped for the open air ministry.

In these days Hull Fair was an important venue in the itinerary of the Open Air Mission, though it was a difficult assignment. Here Willie Docherty describes the situation in his own words: "Open Air Mission evangelists would say that at Hull Fair, people would come in and just walk past them in their thousands. Well, I made up my mind that if we were going to be there, then people were not just going to walk past us." This was a brave statement, but perhaps

25

easier said than done. However, nothing daunted, Willie introduced Raymond, who, slinging the old accordion over his shoulder, led off into an old Gospel chorus, "It was a grand day when I was born again."

Unsophisticated and simplistic though it was, the duet nevertheless stopped many as they flooded into the Fair, and so the basic necessity for the open air preacher of gathering a crowd, was successfully achieved with a minimum of fuss. Anyone who saw the masterly way that Raymond utilised these means in his later ministry would recognise that he had learnt his trade well. Listen to Willie again as he assesses the ability of Raymond in these early days of their ministry together: "He had the gift of the orator without a shadow of doubt, and if he had not been converted he would certainly have made his way profitably on the political platform because the natural gift was there."

The challenge of living and working together harmoniously and sacrificially in confined circumstances has sadly not always been the hallmark of Christian service. The most wonderful gifts and abilities can turn sour in the process of living and working together. Not so with Raymond and Willie. The work of the Open Air Mission, involving as it did, so much travel, constant output, disrupted lifestyle, minimal financial return, great lack of privacy; all these produced a certain stress factor which found out the true temper of a man. Willie and Raymond had five glorious years which each could testify were the best of their lives.

1952 in Trafalgar Square, London, one of the great centres of international tourism worldwide, highlights one of the reasons why both men could assert that these Open Air Mission years were so precious to them. The reason for the first visit to the famous landmark was the occasion of the Centenary of the Mission. What better venue in all the nation than this thronging centre of attraction in the great Metropolis!

With what trepidation, yet anticipation, the evangelists approached the day. Arriving around 3 o'clock in the afternoon, they soon had the familiar but effective routine going, and the crowds began, not just to gather but to amass. Willie, as ever the able strategist in assembling the crowd, finally handed over to Raymond when literally hundreds of people were standing within hearing distance.

The unique element that distinguishes the master craftsman in the open air arena from the "run of the mill" worker, is the ability not only to hold the crowd, but to add to it. Even in these early days of Raymond's career, this ability manifested to an unusual degree and the crowd was largely held spellbound. They were humoured, they were challenged, they were cajoled, were pleaded with like some great conductor with a mighty symphony orchestra under complete control, so Raymond created a sublime tapestry of Gospel words which funnelled the massive audience from the broad highways of Vanity Fair, to the narrow, blood-stained way of the Cross of Calvary. Like some magical Pied Piper, he drew them and they followed on. The Holy Spirit brooded over the event to convict in sovereign power. What was the secret of this charisma, this authority over that most un-predictable of entities, the "non-captive" audience? No obligation detained those hundreds who listened. Indeed, Raymond often said, "Your feet are not nailed to the ground — you can go if you wish." But they seldom did. Here surely is cause for sober reflection by any concerned to communicate the Gospel. Would our presentation, unction, sincerity, compassion, detain a "non captive" audience? A unique gift of God — yes! The accompaniment of the Holy Spirit — undoubtedly. But still, there are principles and elements employed by master craftsmen that are worthy of serious consideration by all concerned preachers. Today especially, the pre-dominant situation in evangelism is a formally arranged gathering, the preacher is cossetted with the predictable "captive audience." Good manners, courtesy, the fear of man, these often detain the hearers rather than the power of God, or the special ability or excellence of the preacher. God was with Raymond!

Annual visits to Manchester by the Open Air Mission took Willie and Raymond to the unlikely location of a Second World War bomb site. Unlikely or not, from Monday till Friday they toiled in the Gospel throughout the month of February. Contrary to general foreboding, the Manchester "monsoon" did nothing to dampen the big attendances at the lunch-time meetings.

And so they came, businessmen, shop assistants, office workers, a great cross-section of the population. As the week progressed so the crowds increased. Before the week was over four or five hundred congregated. Characters, incidents, anecdotes, tales legendary and apocryphal proliferate around such a ministry. Happily we have Willie Docherty's personal recollections of some of Raymond's rapier thrusts to the ever-present hecklers who are constantly magnetised to such meetings. Their remarks could be humorous, provocative, blasphemous or totally irrelevant, but Raymond was seldom, if ever, beaten!

A "wee" Jewish Master Tailor attached himself to the bomb site meetings and seemed somehow convinced that his regular chant that, "He made trousers!" was of some religious or spiritual significance. This was an inference, suggesting that he worked but the preachers were layabouts. After being assailed with this interruption on several occasions, Raymond at the appropriate moment, fixed upon him intently and exclaimed, "Mister, you make the trousers, but I wear them and keep you in a job." This received the approval of the huge crowd and vanquished the "wee Jew!"

The bomb site was directly opposite Boots the Chemist, whose flickering neon sign proudly proclaimed, "Open 24 Hours a Day." Another heckler whose persistent harangue was an irritation to all, was a woman of ill repute. The "Madam" of several prostitutes, she bitterly and constantly poured out her inane objections. Finally with some exasperation, Raymond rounded on her and declared, "Missus, your mouth reminds me of Boots the Chemist, open 24 hours a day!"

The euphoria which greeted VE day and the subsequent immediate election of a Labour Government with a sweeping majority had begun to subside. The Iron Curtain was strung across Europe. Russia blockaded West Berlin. Identity Cards and Ration Books were still a reminder of the grim austerity of the war years. It was a time of re-alignment for the emerging generation. The Atom Bomb had restrained the outburst of sheer pleasure seeking that might have been expected to follow such a dark conflict. The "Swinging Sixties" would perhaps provide that belated opportunity.

In the meantime, there was a people who had to contend with a longer period of frustration before the "bright new world" dawned. The nation had paid dearly; it had a crippling debt to the United States, and had been stripped of most of its foreign assets. Still, there seemed to be a kind of buoyant hope. Many who gathered at these open meetings were maybe unconsciously seeking to establish if that hope was somehow encapsulated in the preacher's message.

Raymond loved the more personal aspect of speaking and debating with students, and, particularly at Hull, young people attending University and College were attracted to the cut and thrust of debate and also the wise counsel that Raymond brought. He possessed a maturity beyond his years, which may not have been apprehended by casual observation. The unfortunate pseudo intellectuals who tried to air their knowledge, or patronise this apparently archetypal working class artisan, usually retired sadder but wiser individuals. However, it must be recorded that Raymond always dispensed wisdom or engaged in debate in a courteous and gentlemanly fashion, so that those whose arguments or objections were not sustained did not generally feel aggrieved.

Henry Gilpin, or "Harry" as he was known to his compatriots in the Open Air Mission, was an Irishman of Methodist farming stock. It seemed appropriate somehow, that an Irishman should join a Scotsman and a hybrid Scots/Irish evangelist in the Open Air Mission caravan. Harry, the new recruit drafted to work with Willie and Raymond, remembered his introduction to the two worthies in this way: "I applied for membership of the Open Air Mission in January, 1951, and reported to the headquarters in John Street, London, where I was sent to Reading to join two evangelists already working in a campaign based in a local Congregational church. The two evangelists were Willie Docherty and Ray McKeown.

Harry had two years of Bible College training, but this was his first assignment as a full-time Christian worker. Willie and Raymond awaited the arrival of their new co-worker with some interest and speculation, especially in light of the fact that there were only two beds in the caravan! Normally two workers shared a caravan but there happened to be no vacancy available at this particular time with any other evangelist. Harry laid a mattress between the beds and thus began their temporary but happy association.

The rough and tumble of caravan life soon integrated the "Three Musketeers" and Harry remembers an occasion when they inadvertently ran out of food one Saturday evening. "Someone kindly gifted us a basket of eggs, so we had two fried eggs for breakfast, lunch, dinner and supper without even a piece of bread to accompany the fare."

Again in his own words, Harry recalled an incident which shows something of the humour and ingenuity displayed by his companions: "One of the big problems as you can imagine with men in a caravan, is laundry. As you used a shirt and it got dirty you put on another, likewise socks and underclothes, so that it soon started to pile up. Me, being the 'greenhorn,' I asked Willie and Ray, what do you do about this? because there's a bit of a problem here.

29

'Not at all Harry, you just leave it to us!' But they didn't disclose what they were going to do. Time was going on, and in the course of the campaign, they announced that there was going to be a slide lecture on Gospel excuses relating to 'Why I am not a Christian'.

The night duly arrived, the lights were dimmed and Ray and Willie projected the slides with suitable comments.

After a series of slides which included such titles as "There are too many hypocrites in the church" which showed people with their noses up in the air in a disdainful fashion, the evangelists eventually arrived at the final slide entitled, "I'm doing the best I can." This showed a man up to his elbows in soap suds in a tub, trying to wash his clothes. This slide received more time and explanation than any of the others. Now while Willie described the slide, Raymond prayed hard that the Lord would apply the message. "Here's a man trying to wash his own clothes and he's doing the best he can but it's not good enough." Willie emphasised this a lot.

At the end of the service when shaking hands with the folks going out, an innocent old lady came up and said, "Excuse me, do you mind if I ask you a very personal question?"

"Not at all," Willie and Raymond responded.

"Well," she asked, "What do you do about your laundry?"

The message had gone home, "We went into that caravan and got a bag so full of dirty laundry that it was standing by itself in a corner, and the old dear took it home to wash, and that was the answer to the question!"

After an initial spell with Willie and Raymond, Harry was posted to a more permanent situation with another evangelist. However, he still went to Largs every summer to work with his two old mates in the annual seaside meetings on the promenade. This famous Scottish Clydeside holiday resort was an extremely popular family venue in those days. The whole of the Open Air Mission Team also came together every year for the Racecourse open air meetings beginning at Aintree with the Grand National, Chester in May, the Derby at Epsom in June, Royal Ascot in June and the St. Leger at Doncaster in September.

Willie and Raymond were soon to part company in the most harmonious and affectionate manner to pursue their own particular ministries. Harry Gilpin was sent to Glasgow to join Raymond who was then operating from his mother's home in Househillwood. The caravan went out from there to various locations around Glasgow and Harry was introduced to Raymond's beloved open air scene in his native city, which forever occupied a special place in his heart. Glasgow Cross, the Barrows, Pitt Street, the shipyard gates, these were the battle honours in the heyday of open air evangelism ministry. Harry was present to witness and accompany probably one of the finest open air preachers in the Gospel history of Scotland. Indeed it was no exaggeration to say that Raymond was possibly the greatest open air preacher in the United Kingdom in his day.

Numerous forays were made to England by Raymond and Harry, and often culminated in pilgrimage to that shrine of open air preachers, Hyde Park Corner. One of the evangelists would read some New Testament story, and the other would interject with questions which gradually drew a crowd, and when the inevitable heckling arose, Raymond, in his element, thrived in the verbal combat with the assembled crowd.

1953 was the year of the Coronation, the year sweet rationing ended. Food rationing followed suit in 1954, finally to erase those memories of wartime deprivation. The combined forces of the Open Air Mission caravans were at Epsom Downs when Gordon Richards won the Derby on Pinza. The Korean War at last came to an end that year, after escalating to the stage where China had entered the fray. The Mission directed Raymond and Harry to explore the possibility of conducting an outreach in Northern Ireland, and although not the first time that the Mission had operated there, they certainly had not been in the Province for several years.

So, commencing a series of evangelistic meetings in Enniskillen, then to Londonderry, Portrush, Coleraine, where the caravan was placed in the main street for after-church meetings. Many young people were strolling around and stopped to listen as the two men preached without "frills" or added entertainment. One young man was converted and subsequently joined the Salvation Army as an enthusiastic believer. Many factory gates were the scene of open air meetings and hundreds were exposed to the truth of the Gospel at these simple gatherings. Conducting a service in an Independent Baptist Church in Ballymena for Mr. Paisley, they met his son Ian for the first time and established a lasting relationship in the Gospel, although they could never have dreamed that he would become the internationally known figure that he now is.

Back in England in Coronation year, from Tower Hill, London, another landmark site of Gospel evangelists, to the Royal Fleet Review at Portsmouth, the wandering preachers were continually on the move. Life was not always easy and opposition was not unknown in the propagation of the Gospel. Harry recalled one incident at Chester Racecourse. Willie Docherty was preaching up on the little stand which they used as a platform, when two "heavy" gentlemen wearing stewards' uniforms approached and paused on the fringe of the crowd. Willie and the others thought they had come to listen and so they warmed to the task of declaring the Gospel, but the men suddenly rushed forward and hauled Willie bodily off the stand, and then carried the platform away.

One of the leaders of the Mission went to intervene and demanded to see the Clerk of the Course, because they had written permission to be on the site. The stewards agreed to take him to the boss and led him through the main gate whereupon they quickly jumped back inside and left the disconsolate soul locked outside! The Mission went back to the course the following day and carried on as usual. Near the conclusion of the day, Harry spotted one of the offending stewards. He went over and directly confronted the man with his extreme disapproval of the previous day's conduct. Somewhat abashed at the surprise of the encounter, and, being on his own, the fellow blustered and was a little put out. Harry said, "We'll be unlikely to meet again here, but remember that we will all have to meet God, and you will doubtless have to give an account of your actions to His servants yesterday."

Harry came to Largs in 1955 to join Willie and Raymond for what was the last time they would work together. Raymond felt that his abilities could be better utilised if he returned to his trade as a joiner and concentrated on the open air work around Glasgow. "He displayed another remarkable gift," Harry recalled, which was typified on the sea front at Large when engaging in children's meetings in the morning sessions. "There used to be a Punch and Judy man, and you know what kids are for Punch and Judy. Well, this Punch and Judy man would set up just near the caravan and, without fail, Raymond would draw every last one of the kids from the puppets to the Gospel meeting. He had a tremendous way with children."

But the end of the era was coming, and Harry felt that several factors contributed to Raymond's decision to finish his time with the Mission. Their approach was a bit antiquated and hidebound, but more important, winter seasons were always a problem. The evangelists were often away from home in bad weather conditions and had cause to reflect on whether this particular aspect of the work was really profitable. They could be detailed to go off to places like Carlisle without pre-arrangement, and were supposed to find something profitable to do in freezing conditions, or wet rainy weather, and this was often difficult, to say the least. Raymond was never happy if engaged in any activity related to "drumming up" support for the Mission, however much of a necessity this might be.

So by prayer and a variety of providential circumstances, Raymond was gradually convinced that he might be more fruitfully employed by adopting the "tent ministry" principle of the Apostle Paul. In other words, ministering from home, while being engaged at his trade, and reaching his fellow citizens with the Gospel in their workaday environment. He also felt that it was telling in a degree to be able to assert that he came to them at the shipyard and factory gates as one of themselves, a fellow worker and not someone specially paid for the task.

Seeking confirmation from God that this was in accord with the Divine mind, Raymond asked that some able musicians and dedicated open air workers might be brought into contact with him. This prayerful request was adequately answered and Raymond had all the spiritual impetus required to begin a noteworthy chaper in Gospel ministry in Scotland.

Chapter 4

Open Air Work in Glasgow

Wee Bobby Hamilton stirred after a fitful night's sleep. Sunday morning did not usually find him in the best condition. Having a "booze up" on Saturday night was a way of life, something to look forward to after a hard week working as a storeman for the Clyde Port Authority. Supervising the loading of trucks with tons of cement was the kind of occupation that demanded some light relief. "Seems like a nice day," he thought, as the possibility of rising from his bed began to dawn on his consciousness. Mind you, there was not really all that much to get up for. Living in "digs," as he had since he was fifteen years old, did not provide the kind of incentive to greet a new day with marked enthusiasm, especially when suffering from a hangover!

As he got to the point of having a wash and shave, it suddenly occurred to him that this was Sunday again. Now Sunday had been providing a little diversion since he had come across that open air meeting at Glasgow Cross. Warming to the prospect, he remembered how he had enjoyed ridiculing the preacher and mocking the Gospel propositions he had made. "Yes," he mused, "It wasn't a bad day either, and at least he could be somebody when heckling the 'Hallelujahs'!" It was about 2.30 on Sunday afternoon when Bobby Hamilton left Stonend Street in Possilpark, to walk down to Glasgow Cross for some entertainment at the open air meeting.

Sunday was a busy day for Raymond McKeown. There was seldom a Sunday that he was not preaching in various churches throughout the city. There were the regular open air meetings at Glasgow Cross, Barrowland Market, Pitt Street, and often an evening church service as well. To lesser mortals it was a daunting prospect. Hurrying off after a hasty breakfast, Raymond paused long enough to tell Violet that he would be back some time around one for lunch.

One of the boys from the open air team came along in the old green Bedford van to go to the meeting at Glasgow Cross. It came to Raymond, as he prepared to go downstairs to Dumbarton Road, to meet the van, that there had been a "scruffy wee individual" hanging around the Cross for the past few Sundays. Just as the van drew up, Raymond momentarily prayed that God would bless their labours today, and he wondered if the "wee man" would vocalise his opposition as he had done recently.

With one or two of the open air team already in the van, and the pile of equipment, amplifier, microphone stands and speakers rattling in the back, Raymond dismissed the thought of the "scruffy wee man" from his mind to concentrate, as they lurched along Argyle Street, on the more immediate task of pondering some theme to expound for that particular day. Just before arriving at the familiar site of the open air, in the shadow of the old Tron steeple at Glasgow Cross, Raymond had settled the question of the subject to be preached at this meeting. Now that he had resolved what the Gospel emphasis would be, he let his mind rest in preparation, and indeed that was all that was needed, because the years of experience, prayerful dedication allied to an uncommon gift of communication, would do the rest.

The green van parked adjacent to the steeple, sagged lop-sidedly on its protesting springs, as a considerable number of team members crowded in for the prayer time that always preceded the actual open air meeting. The unction of the Spirit, the wisdom of God and penetrating conviction of the Word, were most earnestly sought, as, one after another fervently petitioned the Lord for His Divine help in declaring the Gospel.

The crew extracted themselves from the van, and Raymond reflected as he watched them, on how God had wonderfully answered his prayers that He would send accomplished musicians and dedicated workers, if he meant His servant to pursue the open air ministry in Glasgow. What a collection they were!

An interested crowd began to assemble and watch with some curiosity as all manner of musical instruments and equipment began to be set up. There was Bob Hamilton who had played sax and clarinet for some of the top dance and jazz bands accompanying the legendary Ella Fitzgerald, one of the jazz "greats" of the century. Bob Handyside, who had played piano with several big bands around the country was at that moment strapping an accordion around himself as he joked with some of the others. There was a selection of trumpets led by Willie Massie. The guitars were prominent too, Davie Lawson and John Leach being among the regulars who made up that section. Behind this impressive aggregation there was even a full kit of drums played by an ex semi-professional dance band drummer. Some singers were standing on the perimeter of the group, while Raymond picked up a battered old trombone, which he affectionately called his "Shove me off the pavement." Now Bob Hamilton nodded to set the tempo with a lively "One, two, three, four!." And the band swung into an up-tempo rendering of "Hold the Fort!"

Raymond, many years later, broadcast a series of talks on "Downtown Radio" in Belfast, and this is an interesting look at the transcript of the first of the broadcasts which were entitled "Just a Moment." These little talks described something of the scene we have just considered, and how the team came together, as well as outlining the testimonies of some of the leading participants.

"Had you passed the steeple at Glasgow Cross between the hours of 3 and 4 any Sunday afternoon in the '60's and '70's or visited Glasgow's famous Barrowland Market an hour later, you may have seen and heard something which would have left you puzzled. Accordion, Clarinet, Trumpet, Guitar and Drums playing, not the trad jazz with which such a combo is usually associated, but a hymn like 'The Old Rugged Cross' or 'Abide With Me.' How did it all originate?

Some years before, a wee Glasgow joiner, not particularly interested in churches or religion, heard a preacher called Jock Troup at Glasgow Cross one very cold evening, speaking in very understandable terms about what faith in Christ meant. Working as he did in shipyards and on building sites, the joiner appreciated the fact that a preacher had left the warmth, comfort and safety of a hall to venture into the rough and tumble of a Glasgow street to make his faith known. The joiner came to know Christ himself, and from that moment allied himself with open air preachers.

He found an accordion and an old Gospel hymn were appreciated by a Glasgow crowd, so he ventured forth to face the man in the street with the Gospel in song and word. The people listened sympathetically — folks who, like himself before his conversion, would hardly ever go near a church. He found they loved the old hymns, 'It Is No Secret,' 'What a Friend We Have In Jesus,' simple hymns with a profound meaning. The people also appreciated the message of Jesus put simply and plainly in the vernacular.

36

He even began to pray and ask God to send others to help in the Work. He never guessed that this simple prayer would be answered so wonderfully, perhaps on subsequent mornings you would like to be introduced to these musiciains.''

Wee Bobby Hamilton was just about within sight of Glasgow Cross, passing down High Street at the Royal infirmary, and quite enjoying the walk, for it was a lovely sunny October day in 1960. Although he was now feeling somewhat more invigorated by the stroll in the crisp Autumn Air, yet deep inside he was angry and frustrated, and some of the resentment would be vented at these Christians who knew nothing about the harsh realities of life. He was now abreast of Provand's Lordship, the oldest house in Glasgow, and as he continued down High Street, anger, sorrow and frustration suddenly crystalised into a childhood nightmare, forever etched in his deeply scarred innermost being.

Raglan Street, just off Woodside Road, was his early home. His mother was a Christian who had been converted through the ministry of Seth Sykes, the well known old-time evangelist. Wee Bobby had a speech impediment owing to a palate defect, but his mother's loving care and attention helped him through his youthful schooldays without undue upset. He also had a family name, Bruce (and this is what his own immediate family called him). The memory of this triggered his imagination as he continued to wend his way down High Street, oblivious of his surroundings. He was a seven-year-old boy again, running into his mother's room in Raglan Street and finding her very ill and close to death. He remembered his anguished enquiry as to where she was going, for the mysteries of hospitals and necessity of separation were too much for a child's mind to grasp. "Bruce," she said, "never mind now, God will take care of you."

After his mother died, it was not too long before his father married a woman who was a Roman Catholic. Things did not work out; it was a bad match. Bobby felt the surge of rage and hatred well up within him as he recalled how his Stepmother had torn up a precious photograph of his mother. He remembered how he and his elder brother had physically attacked her in a fury over this despicable act. But the horror of the skin being flayed off his back as his stepmother wielded a heavy stick, was an un-dying memory.

"Maybe the worst of all," he thought, now becoming somewhat morose and belligerent at its very recall, "Maybe the worst of all was the begging. I'd love to ask these 'Hallelujahs': 'Have you ever

37

had to beg for your dinner'?'' He could taste the bitter dregs of that humiliation as sharply today as he did thirty years ago when it was first inflicted.

A drunken brute of a father, a stepmother who hated his guts. You either swallowed your pride and begged or you starved. He thought of the sting of shame as he regularly visited his aunt with a jug for some soup to keep the hunger at bay. Although inexpressed as such, the terrible reality since his mother's death, of never being the object of even a speck of love, permeated every fibre of his being. This fact continually fuelled the resentment and grudge he felt against society in general.

High Street and Argyle Street, were two main arteries that channelled people on Sunday afternoons toward the ''Barrows.'' The ''Barrows'' were an institution to Glaswegians, who were normally quite shrewd and astute in business matters but somehow lost all sense of proportion when they came under the spell of the various vendors and innumerable stalls which constituted the magnetic ''mecca'' of Sunday afternoon shoppers. ''Never mind the quality, feel the width!'' summed up the kind of wheeling and dealing that took place. Everybody knew it, but nobody cared. ''Jimmy's the name, and selling's the game! There was no place like the ''Barras!''

Wee Bobby was now walking in this stream of humanity, mingling with the animated crowd intent on a pleasant afternoon's shopping. Physically he was there, but mentally he was still lost in reverie. He was at home, alone, in Raglan Street, when the moment he continually dreaded suddenly arrived. His father burst in through the door, unsteady and bleary-eyed from his constant drinking bouts.

''What's wrong with snivelling Bruce today?'' he snarled.

Knowing what to expect, wee Bobby, then 12 years old, cowered terrified in a corner, and when his drunken father lunged toward him he involuntarily raised his hands in self-defence.

''You can't even talk to me right,'' he raged, ''and you want to fight me, do you?''

So, he locked the door and reeled over to his son and began to punch and kick him insensible. ''He nearly killed me,'' Bobby thought, ''And I was almost fifteen before I got out of hospital and looked for lodgings to escape the nightmare.

Yes, I've had to struggle for survival every day since, I've had to learn fast, become wise in the city's concrete jungle, fend for myself, and what I've learned the hard way. If anybody gets in my way I'll trample over them, beat them up, kick them, cheat them, lie to them, use them, I've learnt the law of the jungle where the weakest go to the wall. Nobody has got anything to teach me about life, especially 'Hallelujahs'!''

Suddenly he was brought back to earth by the opening sound of the big band at the Cross. Realising that he had covered the last half-mile or so in deep thought and troubled emotion, he found a place at the back of the large crowd, which, attracted by the lively music, was growing steadily.

"Let's see if they can teach wee Bobby anything about life, anything that he hasn't learned the hard way."

But mingled with the note of defiance, there was a cry from the heart, unrecognised as such maybe, but nevertheless the cry of a desperately needy soul, a cry for just a mite of genuine love in the awful desolation of such a lonely existence. Already, however, that need had been totally met in a past eternity by the Sovereign God, and Divine Providence was about to realise in time, what God had decreed from everlasting ages.

"What a glorious day," Raymond was inwardly praising God for the weather, and the large crowd which was gathering. The musicians were blasting out the old Gospel hymns to the glory of God. The Lord had answered his prayers and he could scarce take it in. Big Bob Hamilton was at the front now his eyes closed, head tilted back and the clarinet pointed heavenward as he rendered a virtuoso performance of "The Old Rugged Cross." The Glasgow crowd loved it, for this hymn never failed to melt their hearts. Even the odd drunk that always seemed attracted to such gatherings, lustily joined in the chorus in what he considered were dulcet tones. Raymond himself, was now at the microphone with the familiar old accordion strapped on, singing in an excellent tenor voice, "I have a Shepherd, one I love so well." The weather was perfect and the band in great form, the crowd good-humoured — what an opportunity to bait the hook with the Gospel and bring them face to face with the realities of Jesus Christ and Him crucified!

"God has given us a marvellous platform to preach from today," thought Raymond, and his soul was fired and energised by the Holy Spirit for the task at hand.

There was an invasion some years later into Gospel service, of a practice that was never seen, neither would have been tolerated at these services. It is the now all too common practice of applause being rendered, especially by Christians, for singing or musical contributions in the evangelical sphere. Some of the participants at Glasgow Cross had tasted of the heady intoxication of the applause of men and needed no admonition as to the inadvisability of such a custom in the service of one who declared "I will not share my glory with another."

Wee Bobby, leaning against the frontage of the bank at the back of the crowd, became increasingly interested in the proceedings when Raymond called on Bob Hamilton to say something regarding his conversion to Christ. The fact that they both had the same name stimulated wee Bobby's interest. Bob Hamilton began to tell of the life of a professional dance band musician and its attendant temptations and problems. With real conviction and sincerity, he recounted how that when he took his first drink, he had no intention of becoming an alcoholic. This struck a responsive chord in his namesake as he listened, because excessive drinking was one of his major problems. Bob went on to tell how a Harley Street specialist had given him three weeks to live unless some radical change took place in his lifestyle.

The dramatic conversion experience one night in his own home, and subsequent immediate deliverance from the power of drink and of sin in general which he related, came home to wee Bobby with some force. Bob Hamilton had a favourite verse of Scripture which he concluded his address by quoting, "Therefore, if any man be in Christ, he is a new creature: old things are passed away; behold, all things become new."

It was not just wee Bobby who was impressed by this testimony, but many of the crowd who also had drink related problems, recognised in the shining face and total commitment to Christ manifested by this completely changed man, a shaft of hope in the cul-de-sac of dark imprisonment that their own sin perpetually fashioned, shutting them in to continuing misery and dismal hopelessness.

Wee Bobby found his mind now drifting back to recall a godly mother who had also professed what these men were declaring, and there was no denying that she was the only human being for whom he had ever had the slightest regard. At this point, Raymond announced that a young couple would accompany themselves on the guitar and sing a Gospel song before he brought the closing message for the day.

Chapter 5

A Remarkable Conversion

Raymond began to sum up the events of the afternoon as the winter sun still lingered, casting its shadow over the Tron steeple. Wee Bobby shifted a little uneasily as he listened, having the strange feeling that the preacher was speaking directly to him with a peculiar knowledge and insight of his present state and condition. "This Gospel is not 'pie in the sky' when you die, but something practical that has worked, as you have been hearing, in the life of a building site labourer, a nurse, a joiner, something that has the power to take men and women to the farthest outposts of the globe to care for their fellows. It's penetrated prisons and spoken to men who were the enemies of society, saved them, and made them friends of the Lord Jesus Christ, made them love those they once hated and abused."

Rising to a crescendo, Raymond challenged the hushed crowd, "In the name of God, friends, is that practical enough for you? Are you still going to go from here and tell us that Christianity is not relevant, not up to date, it's not for 1960? Are you going to come and tell us that these folks who have come here to this meeting, an ex-professional musician, a sales representative, a lift engineer, those others in the band and some who are standing around praying, are you going to tell us that they all came here at their own expense, some from quite a distance, to tell you a bundle of lies? What good would it do them, let me ask you friend, what good would it do them?

Nobody has come and shoved a bag under your nose looking for a collection. We've never taken a penny from anyone in our life and we're not going to start now. So it's not paying us financially, and if you get converted and ask the Lord Jesus into your life, we're not one whit interested in what church you go to. If you trust the Lord Jesus Christ, what you do after that is between you and God. So we're not out here to try to get you to join our denomination.

Whether we ever see you face to face again is a matter of indifference to us. We are out here to introduce you to our Lord Jesus Christ. We tell you that it is not Protestantism or Roman Catholicism that's the answer to your needs; the answer to your need is neither in minister or priest, nor in Archbishop nor in Pope. The answer to your need is in a living person who died for sinners like you, who rose again from the dead and is alive today and right now can invade that life of yours, and make you an absolutely new creature in Christ Jesus.''

"How much does it cost? I was an apprentice joiner when I got saved, I didn't have much in my pocket, no I didn't have much left in my pocket when I paid my mother for my keep, but it cost me absolutely nothing! I tell you this, my friends, I tell you this, no matter what uniform a man wears, or what titles he has, if he mentions salvation and money in the same breath, he's an impostor. God's salvation is free. You can do nothing to buy it. God offers the sinner salvation right here, right now, without money and without price, and the Word of God empowers us to come to Glasgow Cross and proclaim right now, that there is salvation for you here today, without money and without price!''

Wee Bobby was listening intently now, and the concluding remarks in Raymond's message were absolutely apposite to his present need.

"Last week," Raymond continued, "I spoke to some fellows who had been lying out all night, many of them under the influence of cheap wine and the like. The publican and the bookie took every penny from most of them, but it wasn't the publican or the bookie who were down to give them some hot soup and bread for their poverty. No, it was the 'Hallelujah,' showing compassion and talking to them about the Saviour. And, mark well, my friend, if salvation was of money, if you had to pay for it, there would be no salvation for these boys. But I tell you that I read in the Bible time and time again of Christ coming face to face with beggars, and they wouldn't be begging if they had anything in their pocket, would they? — unless they were Chancellor of the Exchequer. Yet the Saviour came and offered to them the very same salvation that he offered Nicodemus, who was a man of quality and substance. You see, friend, when Christ comes to a man, He is not interested in what the man's got, not interested in what the man's got, He's interested in who the man is.''

Wee Bobby found himself gravitating from the back of the crowd to the front, so that he could catch every word and watch the earnestness of the preacher as he touched the very core of Bobby's justification for his rebellion, lying, cheating, alcoholism and truculent disregard for God or man. It was simply that nobody loved him, nobody cared whether he lived or died, but now the preacher was presenting a proposition that seemed unbelievable — there was One who cared, even for such a wretch as he.

Raymond was now completely absorbed in his final declaration. He sensed that the crowd was hanging on to every word, that God was answering many prayers diligently made by himself and the team since the inception of the open air work. Wee Bobby thought. "This man truly loves his God, just like my mother did. If this is true I'd like to believe on this Christ."

Raymond was pleading and challenging, making the final statements penetrate hearts, like arrows from the divine bow. He caught a fleeting glimpse of wee Bobby as his eyes scanned the motionless crowd. At that moment he was unaware of the divine transaction taking place in the wee man's heart. "Can you tell me anybody," Raymond pressed the words home, "Can you tell me anybody nowadays who's prepared to love the very worst for themselves alone, and for no other reason? That's our Saviour. That's who we come proclaiming today. That's who we come telling you about this afternoon — a Saviour who can save you without money and without price, and we invite you to come to Him this afternoon, right where you are."

A final hymn was sung and Raymond, coming to the microphone, said, "Now we have a little booklet here called 'Safety, Certainty and Enjoyment.' It's absolutely free to you if you'll do one thing — if you'll promise to read it. If you'll just come forward and take it from my hand, we won't ask any questions, take your name or address, or embarrass you in any way. So they came, a good cross section of Glasgow folks, both young and old, quietly making their way out into the middle of the ring, taking the booklet from the preacher's hand.

It is interesting to note that this was all the "appeal" that Raymond ever felt at liberty to make. Lengthy or prolonged persuading which accompanies much modern day evangelism, was not part of his Gospel armoury. Being a solid immoveable believer in the old "Doctrines of Grace," the Sovereignty of God was therefore a cardinal tenet of his faith, and he was ever careful to avoid what he considered an intrusion into the work of the Holy Spirit. He had the faith to believe that if he declared a biblical Gospel, well "watered" by prayer, then God would do His own work His own way.

When the meeting was over, Raymond casually looked around the dispersing crowd, but there was no sign of the "wee man." Bobby had left just before the conclusion, his mind in a turmoil. One part of him affirmed the preacher's message, but the other part of him was insidiously saying, "Where was the God of love when your mother died and left a wee boy to fend for himself?" He jostled through the crowds in Argyle Street in the late October afternoon, scarcely noticing the chill of evening as it descended rapidly on the shoppers going home from the "Barrows." Again the nagging, persistent voice was speaking within him, "Where was the God of Love when your father kicked a helpless young boy unconscious?" Just beyond the Central Station bridge, he turned up Hope Street and turned left again into Bothwell Street. His mind was in an upheaval as he continued towards Elmbank Street, scarcely looking to left or right, and he had no need to for this was a habitual Sunday evening exercise, moreover, the drink he would consume in the Working Men's Club tonight would be especially welcome.

"Hello, Bobby, how's things going?" the barman greeted the familiar figure. "Fine, Gimme a large whisky!" wee Bobby replied. He was still in a turmoil over what he had heard, and indeed the part of him that responded to the insidious voice within, was seething at this McKeown fellow, with his "God of Love" message. Suddenly he threw down the money for the drink, turned on his heel and strode to the front door. The doorman was astounded. "Bobby," he cried, "I never thought I'd live to see the day that you walked in here sober, and walked out the same way! What's wrong with you? Are you ill?" Usually the doorman had to fetch a taxi to take the drunken "wee man" home, but tonight Bobby was striding out "cold sober." The doorman shook his head in disbelief at the departing figure and retreated to the bar to discuss this phenomenon with the barman. Could this be the same wee "hard man" who could lift a half bottle of whisky to his mouth, and dispose of it with one long swig?

When Bobby finally arrived back at his lodgings in Stonend Street, Possil, it seemed to him that this was the longest day he could remember in his whole life. "Was it really only this afternoon that he had set out for the open air meeting?'' It seemed an eternity, yet paradoxically, it also seemed to compress into a fleeting second, a kaleidoscope of vivid images pulsating through his mind. In this bemused state, wee Bobby stumbled into his own room and fell on his face and wept. How long he wept he could not recall, but interspersed with the sobs was the cry, ''God, that fellow McKeown says if I call on you in earnest, you'll save me. Even though I've turned my back on you, even though I've called you all the wicked names under the sun, oh, God, that man says you can still love me. Lord I don't know any prayers. All I know is that I need you and I'm coming to you, and I'm asking you, could you find it in your love to forgive me, cleanse me and come into my heart right now?''

Bobby explained the effect of this event in his own words: ''In my wee room it was like it lit up, and a peace surged into my soul that I'd never known in my life before. The agitation, the aggression was gone and for the first time in years I laid my head on the pillow and slept without taking sleeping tablets. On Monday morning I set out to go to work, but this time I set out without my handful of tranquilisers.''

It was only a quarter of a mile along the Gallowgate to the ''Barrows'' and when the ''open air'' finished at Glasgow Cross, the boys quickly got the gear and instruments packed away, so that they could get round to Barrowland as soon as possible. Raymond, like the others, sometimes walked round, sometimes went in the van. The open air meeting at the ''Barrows'' was different in character from the one at Glasgow Cross. There was a kind of natural stance at the Cross in the little slip road around the steeple, which the team ''commandeered'' every Sunday for an hour, at little inconvenience to passing traffic. This meant that they were on the slip road facing the crowd who largely congregated on the pavement. It was an ideal arrangement and provided plenty of room for both participants and hearers.

No such arrangement existed at the ''Barrows.'' The van parked in a fairly narrow street, which was usually thronging with people going or coming to the innumerable stalls, barrows or even mere suitcases spread on the ground before the wary eyes of their vigilant owners. All kind of transactions took place, legitimate, semi-legitimate, and downright dishonest! The drunks were there, pickpockets, criminals, and a large and varied selection of honest Glasgow working class folks, mostly good natured and enjoying the banter and dubious statements of the traders. It was right in the middle of this melee that the open air meeting was set up in Kent Street, which connected London Road with the Gallowgate.

The usual format was employed with the music being utilised to draw the crowd, but at the "Barrows" the musicians and the participants mixed with the hearers, hecklers or passing throng. There was no space for a set up such as the Glasgow Cross meeting and this inter-mingling provided opportunity for the opponents of the Gospel to infiltrate right into the heart of the gathering. Sam was an atheistic "free thinker" who insidiously got alongside young Christians to disturb them regarding Christ and the Word of God. Although Raymond warned the workers regularly not to engage in converse with such as Sam, the young zealots sometimes thought they knew better and eventually had to be rescued when they found themselves trapped by the crafty ploys of seasoned humanists like Sam. Raymond himself had a good relationship with such types and could more than hold his own with them when debating the Gospel.

The Trotskyites, or more radical Socialists (of whom the Militant Tendency are the modern equivalent), were usually bleating away in close proximity, but very few listened or took them seriously. Perhaps an incident that Raymond recalled gives some insight into why this should be. Apparently he had been on a bus one day when one of the radical Socialist orators who occupied a soapbox at the "Barrows," where he regularly implied that he had the remedy for the world's ills, was refused admission to the bus. He proceded to rant and rave with the foulest language imaginable, which caused Raymond to reflect how that a supposed ability to clean up the world was not harnessed to an ability to clean up his own mouth!

Bert Norris, Raymond's brother-in-law, Sam Hamilton, Jackie Boyd and other Christians helped in the open air and often, while they were holding forth, Raymond could regularly be seen cajoling some Christian visitor he had just noticed in the crowd, to testify for Christ or sing a Gospel song to the "Barrows" clientele.

Raymond had very definite ideas on how an open air meeting should be conducted. In his estimation brevity in the speakers was an essential. Very few preachers are ever rebuked for being too short in their orations and Raymond, being well acquainted with this problem, devised a solution in his own inimitable way. When he had requested someone to bring a brief word of testimony, and he inevitably discovered that "brief" was not a word they were conversant with, he took action. After about three minutes, he would strap on the accordion and begin to play very quietly. If the hearing of the object of his attention was defective, he would gradually increase the volume till they got the message. It was an effective device and normally achieved the desired result without recrimination!

The environment of the "Barrows," the nature of the meeting there, the miscellany of people who congregated made the "Hallelujahs" somewhat more susceptible to opposition, both verbal and physical, than at other venues. Sometimes rotten fruit was thrown from somewhere in the crowd or coins would descend from the skies, but not necessarily as a sign of approval. Some vociferous hecklers would hurl verbal abuse, either in passing or from very close range. It was not known for some, usually inebriated, to "eyeball" those who took part by standing immediately in front of the microphone from where they sought to intimidate the preacher or singer, by staring at them aggressively, or insulting them with inane or most profane remarks. These interventions were not generally viewed with much favour by the majority of ordinary decent folks who listened, but, nevertheless, they could prove quite disconcerting for inexperienced speakers, or young ladies who were singing a Gospel song. All such irritations were handled by Raymond with consummate ease, and often to the discomfiture of the perpetrator. One small example illustrates the point.

Raymond's methodology in these type of meetings was to commence with music and singing, intersperse this with testimonies from different Christians, including many who were not members of the recognised open air team. When he came to conclude the meeting with a spontaneous Gospel message, he would start in a low key fashion with some humorous quips, and so have the attendant crowd in a good receptive mood for the serious, though extempore, Gospel message. On this particular occasion, he had remarked that some wiseacre had been telling him that he did not believe in sin. Raymond asked the crowd, "Do any of you have this philosophy? Do you have this belief, Mister?" Looking around the assembled hearers, he then said, "If you do I hope that you're consistent, because you'll never need a joiner like me to come and fix a lock on your door, will you?"

While he was speaking, a young man, who was a Roman Catholic, wearing a "Sacred Heart" badge in his lapel, began to interrupt the meeting with some very foul language which he utilised to underline his opposition to the Gospel message. Raymond turned on him quickly and said, "Sir, if the religion represented by the badge you wear cannot rid you of such a filthy tongue, then get rid of that religion." Murmurs of approval and nods from the bystanders indicated their sympathy with the remarks. This was not unusual, because Raymond had remarkable empathy with working-class folks and they were greatly attracted to him even if they did not subscribe to his evangelical beliefs. Another little example confirms this.

The McKeowns had a rather noisy drunken neighbour, who because of alcoholism, was a regular source of annoyance to them when living in Scotstoun. He was always fighting, swearing, causing a disturbance as he made his way unsteadily to his flat above the McKeown's. Most average folks would have been thoroughly disenchanted with such behaviour and would have doubtless remonstrated with the culprit, or even sent for the police at times. Not so Raymond. He had an unbelieveable "tolerance-level" and such was this effect upon the man, that in his better moments he often came to talk to Raymond like a bosom friend, and thought the world of him. There was something unique, magical in the best sense of the word, in the harmonious relationships that Raymond established with all manner of his contemporaries, a rapport that he seemed to be able to generate with Christian or non Christian alike.

The early Sixties were producing much material that Raymond could utilise in his open air preaching. Pornography was beginning to flood into the country and the deteriorating morality of Britain facilitated the influx of filthy literature, some of which was even imported in the guise of Bibles or educational books. Raymond hated this trade with an intense, single-minded detestation. "Women's Lib" was on the march too, and their condemnation of pornography, or the Miss World beauty contest, as "blatent sexism" was wedded to demands for "Abortion on demand" for all women.

The Great Train Robbery took place in 1963 and 2.5 million pounds in used banknotes went missing. Sin was abounding. When alluding to politicians as neither having the integrity or answers for the real dilemma of the people, Raymond found weight added to his arguments when the "Profumo" scandal erupted, revealing that "call girls" were active in some high places in government.

Changes in age-old values and beliefs were taking place with breath-taking rapidity. The Beatles engulfed the younger generation like an epidemic, "liberating" them into sexual permissiveness and the drug culture. Their message was diametrically opposed to what Raymond was proclaiming to men and women, old or young, in open air meetings, cinema queues, factory gates, churches at work or wherever the opportunity arose. The Beatles said that by the use of drugs a man could find truth within his own self, and that even by psychedelic rock music alone, the same effect might be achieved. What an impetus this gave to Raymond's preaching, because he had once been enthralled by the writings of Huxley the humanist, before Huxley began to advocate the use of drugs in the pursuit of truth "within oneself." Eastern religions were the next logical step in this sequence of thought, because they basically propagated the same message of inward searching.

The perceptive listener at any of Raymond's open air meeting during this period, could trace the emphasis that he made against such heresy as seeking "truth within." He strove to point men away from themselves and to look to Calvary. The very subjective nature of the cultural eruptions of the Sixties, were a defiant blow against the objective principle of the Gospel, but Raymond was well versed in these philosophies, and countered them simply in modern parabolic form, which especially captivated the uninitiated hearer. Here is a brief example of the simple treatment of an everyday incident, so immediately recognisable, that ordinary folks could easily understand the spiritual lessons drawn from the narrative.

Addressing the crowd in Buchanan Street, Glasgow, shopping precinct, Raymond asked, "What's Christianity all about? It's not about patching up old lives, it's about making new ones. I've been a joiner for many years down on Clydeside and daily work from house to house. Do you know one of the things that really annoys housewives? It's when I arrive at the house with a wee bit of wood to repair a window. They say to me, 'Now look, you're not getting into my house to do a patched up job! If that's all you're going to do, off you go and I'll get in touch with my Town Councillor, and I'll see that I get a new window.' Actually they were quite sensible in their attitude, for they were paying their rents and rates and had a right to get proper treatment. But I used to wonder, 'Why is it that they allow their lives to be patched up, and treat them in a way that they would not treat their windows or doors?' You see, when we come out on to the street to speak to you, it's not with a message to help you patch up your life. No! We're telling you that if you'll look away to Jesus and fully trust in Him, He'll give you a brand new life!''

Raymond had a characteristic pose when he was preaching in the open air. He would stand at times, almost side on to the audience, one hand on hip, and the right hand raised heaven-wards, as he emphasised a point. Later when the bushy, untidy hair was grey, and intense earnestness and sincerity often rivetted the hearers, he took on the appearance of an almost prophet-like figure. He also had an ingredient called the "common touch," which is often conspicuously absent, even amongst many well-known preachers. The Saviour displayed this attribute in a matchless way, so that the common people heard Him gladly.

Many modern evangelical ministers espouse the Gospel cause, but sadly often display traits more akin to secular class structure, than primitive Christianity. Out of the pulpit they become un-approachable, patronising, and often project more of the mannerisms of a Pope, than a brother in Christ. Part of Raymond's greatness was due to the fact that he was none of these things, although the gifts and knowledge he possessed could have made lesser men tend to pride. Some of the "leading lights" in evangelical circles did deign to acknowledge him to be a "good brother," but seldom good enough to occupy their platforms, except for minor or insignificant gatherings. Being cloistered in safe, cosy pulpits, and protected from the realities of the outside world by their insular life styles, they had convinced themselves that no prophet or ministry could possibly arise outwith the "status quo" of orthodox church channels.

Being pushed aside, albeit unconsciously, by lesser mortals, was the story of Raymond's life and ministry. A glaring example of this took place in the early Sixties.

There had been a national campaign against pornography and the breakdown of moral standards, which culminated in a series of public meetings in various cities throughout Britain. The meeting in Glasgow was held in George Square in front of the Municipal Buildings. There was representation from the entertainment world and church bodies. Raymond at this time had been conducting a ceaseless and relentless single-handed campaign against pornography, with considerable success in the Glasgow area.

On the night, a large crowd assembled around the magnificently constructed platform, floodlit and garlanded with flowers. Situated on the south side of the Square, with a first-class public address system installed, the dignitaries resplendent in their finery, and seated in places of prominence; it made an impressive sight. That peculiar pretension, sadly often prevalent at evangelistic gatherings, which enables people with very little genuine concern, or limited ability to express such little concern as they have, by "hogging the limelight," was much in evidence on this occasion. Any event likely to attract public attention, suffers in this respect, and this was no exception. The meeting commenced with formal speeches from civic leaders, and splendid singing from professional artistes.

The man who was eminently suited to handle such a situation, the "master craftsman" Raymond McKeown, mingled on the fringe of the crowd as an onlooker, lost amongst the hundreds who attended the event. What a golden opportunity it would have been for the man with the outstanding gift of oratory, especially in open-air ministry. Not only so, but the man with a tremendous burden and determination, to fight tenaciously against the pornography trade as Raymond had done for many years. It must be recorded, and his closest associates could affirm, that they never heard an egotistical statement emanate from him, nor indeed any complaint made with regard to numerous occasions when similar incidents arose which must have been somewhat frustrating and provocative to him.

Chapter 6

Some Unique Incidents

Wee Bobby Hamilton awoke from a peaceful night's sleep and arose with total conviction concerning what had to be done that day. He was not instructed in the Word of God yet, but the Saviour had saved him yesterday, and now Bobby knew that his workmates must hear the good news. When he arrived at the C.P.A. cement yard, he made straight for the little hut that served as the assembling point. There was the usual hubub of conversation going on before the commencement of the day's labour.

Being Monday morning, there was perhaps just a shade more reluctance to begin the week's drudgery, so the men were in no particular hurry to move out. Geordie, one of Bobby's mates, was holding forth in the hut, surrounded by several of his workmates, and his narration was punctuated by some very foul language. "Hey, Geordie," Wee Bobby said. "Just take it easy with that language!" George was somewhat nonplussed, as were the other occupants of the hut, but, thinking it was some kind of sick joke, they carried on unabated. "I said cut out that filthy language," Bobby repeated, every eye now incredulously fixed upon him. "What's wrong with you, have you had another bout of the D.T.'s? they shouted. This produced a gale of ribald laughter and derogatory comments, but wee Bobby went on un-abashed, "No I haven't. I've got converted, I became a Christian at the weekend." This revelation stopped the animated conversation and dispersed the group to their various tasks. They engaged in amazed conversation regarding the bombshell which had just been delivered. "Bobby Hamilton converted?" was the cynical query of one who had arrived just too late to hear the announcement in person. "Bobby Hamilton converted? I'll bet any man a week's wages that it won't last till next pay day."

The following Sunday Bobby set out on his usual stroll from Possilpark to Glasgow Cross with a determination to speak to

Raymond McKeown. This conversation was going to take the breath away from the evangelist. Wee Bobby retraced the steps he had taken on many previous Sundays, but now he was walking tall as a Christian. He could hardly contain himself till he met that man McKeown. Such was his desire to share the news with Raymond that the walk down the High Street had never seemed so long. At last the familiar sight hove in view. There was the old Tron steeple and some of the musicians already tuning up. Bill Queen, the quiet man who twiddled the knobs of the amplifier and generally attended to all the background work, was already bent over the equipment, making last minute adjustments before the opening music commenced.

"Hey, Raymond," wee Bobby shouted, "Hey Raymond! I want to speak to you!" Raymond looked round to see the small shuffling figure approaching with great rapidity. "Can I speak to you?" the wee man said as he came up to him. "Sure," said Raymond, "But what's happened? You look really different, and I can't get used to the fact that you're not shouting abuse at me today. But what's your name and can we do anything for you?"

"Bobby Hamilton," the wee man replied. "Oh, not another one!" Raymond went on humourously, because Bob Hamilton, the ex-professional dance band musician was already a well-known member of the open air team.

"I got saved last Sunday after the meeting," wee Bobby burst out. And, as he related the story, several of the other team members gathered round to introduce themselves and encourage the latest convert.

"Well, we'll have to call you 'wee Bobby' to save confusion," said Raymond. "Now I've got something special for you today. You are going to take a few minutes at the meeting to tell the folks what happened to you last weekend."

Wee Bobby experienced the "butterflies in the stomach" reaction that many of his contemporaries had known as they waited to say something for the Lord at the Glasgow Cross open air meeting. The big crowd looked on with great interest as Raymond announced, "There's a wee fellow here that got saved last week and he's going to take a minute to tell you how it all happened." The fact that Raymond felt confident to throw Bobby in at the "deep end" publicly, after just one week of salvation experience, was an indication of his certainty that God had truly done a work of saving grace in his life. Bobby later was married to Cathy, who, when working as a tram driver, had often recourse to remonstrate with the wee drunk who boarded her tram in an inebriated state. She and Bobby were familiar figures at numerous Gospel meetings conducted by Raymond, and her powerful voice was often used in singing Gospel solos during many years of open air ministry. Raymond's insight regarding wee Bobby's suitability to speak publicly after so short a period of conversion was fully vindicated as the Hamiltons are still serving the Lord after many years.

The McKeowns had two children, Paul and Judith. Just around this time, Paul, who was about seven-years-old, was down in the back court one sunny mid-summer day with his little friend, David, who was five.

One or two folks were taking advantage of a sunny day to sit out and bake in conditions not too common in the wet, grey climate of the West of Scotland. The back courts of Scottish tenement buildings are legendary. It was here that the washing was hung out to dry, children were sent to play, and good days made it a mecca for social gatherings, where neighbours could exchange gossip and discuss the world at large. Paul and his little friend were engaged in animated conversation about school, which wee Dave was shortly to begin attending. Thus it was an innocuous common Glasgow working-class scene, neighbours leaning out of windows, lounging around, chatting, with no sense of any impending catastrophe. Without warning, a huge heavy cast iron offset dislodged from the gutter about fifty feet overhead, and crashed to the ground, striking Paul's little companion on the head, killing him instantly. The pipe rebounded from the child and felled Paul by striking him on the foot, literally breaking every bone. Poor wee Dave was decapitated in gruesome fashion, and Paul was only saved from fatal injury because the offset struck his little friend first. He was immediately rushed off to hospital in a state of shock and pain.

Such was the popularity and vast range of Christian friends the McKeowns knew, that an immediate barrage of prayer was made all over the country, and not only the parents and friends, but the doctors and nurses were amazed at the astoundingly quick recovery and restoration of Paul to normal walking ability. Raymond felt that anything that he sought to do for the Lord was amply repaid by a

God who was no man's debtor, and the Divine intervention in this instance on Paul's behalf, was ample proof of this to him.

Although greatly gifted in many ways above his fellows, and although a high degree of popularity and universal acclaim came his way, Raymond was not without faults and lapses of duty. These occurred in both domestic and public life. One example shows this dereliction of duty in the common round of everyday living. As a joiner, Raymond was competent, if not outstanding, the obvious driving force and passion of his life inhibited any overwhelming interest in the craft of carpentry. One event that occurred illustrates the deficiency perfectly.

Violet had been requesting that various items which needed repair should be attended to by Raymond. One of these items was the swing leg of a dining table which gave her forebodings of disaster because of its precarious and dangerous state. Not even the heavy sarcasm such as, "I really wish I had got married to a joiner," with which Violet assailed him at times, would motivate him. However, his lackadasical ways were to receive a jolt which did most certainly galvanise him into action!

One evening a local Church of the Nazarene minister had been invited to supper. This invitation was made in the midst of continuing procrastination by Raymond over the matter of repairing the table leg. Violet was a little aggravated by this attitude because any other person just had to announce some job that required doing and Raymond gave them quick and cheerful service. As the family sat down to tea, which consisted of large bowls of steaming spaghetti, the reverend gentleman, who was well over six feet tall, was having difficulty in maneouvering his lengthy limbs under the table. The culmination of his deliberate efforts to accomplish this with minimal disturbance, was to receive the bowl of hot spaghetti into his lap, as the offending table leg rapidly gave way. This salutary lesson produced an immediate repair to the table, but did not achieve a lasting amendment to Raymond's rather dilatory domestic ways!

This lack of interest in the mundane things of this world translated itself into the realm of things mechanical also. A car to Raymond was a means of locomotion from A to B, and the mysteries of oil levels, tyre pressures, plugs or points which are fundamental maintenance essentials, did not exist for him. He possessed an ancient Morris Minor whose long suffering ways made it particularly endearing to Raymond. It probably attended more open air meetings in its life span than most evangelical Christians. Some friends of Raymond's in a small fellowship in Clydebank, had noticed that the Minor was growing decidedly "long in the tooth." It was essential that Raymond had reliable transport for the open air work, especially as he traversed the city many days during his lunch-hour to preach at shipyard and factory gates. The Pastor of this fellowship, who was a close friend of Raymond's, decided that something had to be done about the transport situation, and so with the support of the church, a plan was devised.

After much deliberation and prayer, a vehicle which seemed eminently suited to Raymond's scant mechanical knowledge or interest, suggested itself as a possible ideal vehicle. Cameron and Campbell were the Volkswagon agents at this time and were located in Great Western Road near Anniesland Cross. A quick reconnoitre of their showroom revealed a gleaming white one-year-old VW Beetle, in absolutely pristine condition and with low mileage. The church managed to acquire the necessary funds and purchased the vehicle.

Some days later a phone call to Raymond invited the family and himself, to visit the church, whose meetings were held in a house, on some spurious pretext so that he never had the slightest inkling of the true purpose of the invitation. During the course of the evening's fellowship together, the family were invited out by the front door to a large double garage attached to the house, to look at some new open air equipment. The church members, meanwhile, slipped out of the back door and assembled in the darkened garage. When the McKeowns reached the garage doors, the lights were suddenly switched on to reveal around fifty people standing behind a gleaming white VW Beetle, ready to be driven off, thus putting the old Minnor into well earned retirement. No words could describe the look on Raymond's face when the reality of the situation dawned on him, and for once in his life he was speechless! For those onlookers who were responsible for the matter, it seemed a great privilege to be able to do something concrete and helpful for one whose life was dedicated to being so helpful to others. If Raymond had loved the Minor, he was infatuated with the Beetle, and the tales of its long life and reliability became legendary. Like the Morris Minor before it, the Beetle was regularly parked at the Singer sewing machine factory gate, John Brown's Shipyard, Yarrow's Shipyard, Govan

Shipyard, and all the open air sites which Raymond regularly preached at during this time.

As a lover of poetry and music, Raymond utilised these to good effect in widely diversified aspects of Gospel ministry. The "down and out" fraternity were always on his heart, and in between the open air work and the un-ceasing ministry in all kinds of churches, including Church of Scotland, Baptist, Methodist, Nazarene, Brethern, Mission Halls, Pentecostal, he would slip away at odd moments to meet with the derelicts, and cheap wine drinkers, the "drop-outs" of society. He would often be found, for example, in a little Mission on the south side of Glasgow, spending a hurried hour with the unfortunates of society who were largely ignored by the normal evangelical community. Sitting informally in their midst, he would play the old accordion and sing to them while they received some food and a cup of tea. They loved the old Gospel hymns and Raymond's clear tenor voice touched many of their hearts, as did the simple Gospel truths he gave them.

Poetry was also one of his passions, and the works of Robert Burns, Scotland's national poet, were well known to him. He had an unusual gift of utilising one of Burn's poems in certain circumstances which depict his versatility and challenges concerned evangelicals regarding the possibility of effecting a witness for the Saviour on all kinds of occasions. Weddings and funerals give unique opportunities for propagating the Gospel, although they are not always capitalised by Christians as they might be. After-dinner speeches at wedding receptions, often saw Raymond enlist the un-regenerate Scots' particular love of Burns' poetry, to fashion a Gospel message which was at once attractive, and readily acceptable, especially to un-converted folks. He would go about it in this way:

Some introductory humorous remarks, which were always innocuous and disarming, would soon have the guests "eating out of his hand." Although such occasions are not always famed for great oratory, nevertheless, on occasion there were those amongst the guests who could acquit themselves in public speaking. However, once the "master craftsman" slipped into action, people were captivated by the mastery of words, the flashes of wit, and the utter sincerity of the speaker. "Burns," he would say, "Was a remarkable man. For one who was not of the highest moral integrity, he had tremendous insight into things spiritual, as illustrated by these verses from "The Cotter's Saturday Night":

Then kneeling down to Heaven's Eternal King,
The Saint, the Father, and the Husband prays:
Hope springs exulting on triumphant wing,
That thus they all shall meet in future days:
There, bask in uncreated rays,
No more to sigh, or shed the bitter tear,
Together hymning their Creator's praise,
In such society, yet still more dear;
While circling Time moves round in an eternal sphere.

Compar'd with this, how poor Religion's pride,
In all the pomp of method and of art,
When men display to congregations wide,
Devotion's ev'ry grace, except the heart!
The Power, incens'd, the Pageant will desert,
The pompous strain, the sacerdotal stole;
But haply, in some Cottage far apart,
May hear, well pleas'd the language of the Soul;
And in His Book of Life the Inmates poor enrol.

It is not hard to imagine how Raymond could take a couple of lines like:

"Then kneeling down to Heaven's Eternal King,
The Saint, the Father, and the Husband prays:"

and simply point out how that Burns had got the priority of Scripture correct in delineating the Saint first, the Father second, and the Husband last. As a "saint" the man was fulfilling his obligation to pray to His God and Saviour. As a "father," he was priest over his own little congregation, and led them in spiritual exercise before the Lord. And as "husband," he set the example in piety to his family as was his biblical responsibility. A little expansion on these points certainly held the attention of folks who were otherwise uninterested in preaching as such.

The last verse he quoted was designed to gain even more rapt attention, as it touched the fierce patriotism which smoulders in the heart of most Scots. Having painted a picture, in vivid and imaginative terms, of the now merely historical scene of a godly family gathered around the big family bible, he was able to challenge men to recognise that the decline of the nation and the individuals comprising it, could be traced to the departure from such holy exercise. This verse with which he closed the little homily was surely used of God to highlight to sinners the absence of such rectitude in our present frenetic generation.

From scenes like these, old Scotia's grandeur springs,
That makes her lov'd at home, rever'd abroad:
Princes and lords are but the breath of kings,
'An honest man's the noble work of God:'
From scenes like these, old Scotia's grandeur springs,
That makes her lov'd at home, rever'd abroad:
Princes and lords are but the breath of kings,
'An honest man's the noble work of God:'
And certes, in fair Virtue's heavenly road,
The Cottage leaves the Palace far behind:
What is a lordling's pomp? a cumbrous load,
Disguising of the wretch of human kind,
Studied in arts of Hell, in wickedness refin'd!

Spurgeon once said, "A great deal of sermonising may be defined as saying nothing at great length: but out of doors, verbosity is not admired, you must say something and have done with it, and go on to say something more, or your hearers will let you know." Raymond had a remarkable adaptibility which enabled him to accommodate all kinds of circumstances. The keynote was the total reality, without affectation of either word or gesture, which was doubtless nurtured in the arena of the open air, where the niceties of convention and hypocrisy which often pervade the indoor pulpit are singularly absent. He was a master of riposte and spontanaeity, had a completely relaxed approach with an attractive and winsome personality which most folks found irresistable. Poetry, literature and music were great loves of his life, but were not merely indulged in for self-gratification; rather, they were the basis of an expansive knowledge that added interest, colour, variety and humour to his ministry, yet were always framed within sound Reformed theological structure.

Raymond for some years had a latent smouldering desire for revival to come to Scotland in a biblical way. Around the early sixties, through his Tent Hall association he had this simmering desire ignited by a little leprechaun of an Irishman called Tommy Campbell. He was just about the antithesis of Raymond in every way. He was a plain man of little education and devoid of any notable gifts. He had no ministry in preaching, no musical ability and was not well read. But he could pray! As a simple praying godly man he was assured of an affinity with Raymond. Tommy exhibited a one track mind which almost amounted to an obsession, because he ate, drank, slept and lived for revival. Those who knew him had learned that any conversation would rapidly gravitate to the need of national revival. He was a man of God and infected many Christians with a genuine interest to pray for revival around the early '60's. Meetings were convened on Friday evenings in the old Partick Bethel church and also in the Tolbooth Mission. These prayer meetings give wonderful insights into behavioural patterns in Christians and it is worth noting some because they varied from the sublime to the ridiculous.

The meetings commenced around 10.30 p.m. and about thirty or so people would assemble. These could be classified into categories and the classification of individuals was soon established. There were the "meteorites:" they were generally younger believers who had come to make an impression and in the first hour or so they sparkled and shot into heavenly realms with an intensity which brought awe to lesser mortals. After a couple of hours they quickly waned and were heard no more as they quietly slipped away to an early bed. The "gadfly" was another species which was initially attracted to these gatherings, and they were such as visited every new venture with a curiosity which could not be sustained throughout a long night's battle in spiritual warfare on one's knees. They usually dozed off, satisfied in the knowledge that their mere presence had gained them some merit, much as in the Roman Catholic system of indulgences. One humorous incident highlights the dangers of such a practice:

It was the custom to have a short break around 2 a.m. to have a quick cup of tea and a pie to invigorate the warriors, and prepare them for the last session, which usually finished about 6 a.m. On this occasion, a "Gadfly" had settled down on his knees and appeared to be in an attitude of prayer, but had actually fallen asleep. When the time for the break arrived the others quietly slipped up on the pews, and the poor unfortunate "Gadfly" was left in a posture which suggested prayer, but actuallay was one of deep slumber! None of those present sought to enlighten the soul until the gentle buzz of conversation awoke him to the dreaded realisation of his state. The most surreptitious manoeuvres were engaged upon by the hapless individual, and while the onlookers pretended not to notice this exercise, they could scarce suppress the overwhelming desire to have a laugh at the exposure of the "Gadfly."

The category truly worthy of attention is that of the men of spiritual calibre who came to do battle in high places against "principalities and powers." The first hour or so sufficed to flush out any who had only come to spectate. It was an education when Tommy and Raymond and others of like ilk began to lay hold of God for revival. Time was of little consequence, so the intercessions could expand and develop. They consisted of the pleading of various promises relating directly to revival, such as, Isa. 44:3: "I will pour water upon him that is thirsty and floods upon the dry ground. I will pour my spirit upon thy seed, and my blessing upon thine offspring."

On many evenings, when the city of Glasgow slumbered on, the fervent effectual prayers of righteous men ascended to their heavenly Father. The old Hermon Baptist church also became a centre for revival prayer meetings and Raymond often attended there also to join forces in the battle. Sometimes when weariness would almost overtake, particularly in the early morning hours, God would suddenly visit his temple and the flagging spirits of the prayer warriors would be re-energised by the sensible presence of the living God in the midst. Building construction workers, nurses, teachers, salesmen, engineers, policemen, a truly representative cross-section of the community gathered for some years in these meetings. It was not uncommon for some to leave the prayer meeting on a Saturday morning and head off to work, without returning home or having a proper breakfast. Many shades of evangelical opinion were represented, but the common bond of desire for revival seemed to subdue denominational emphasis and blur doctrinal distinctives in the holy quest for an outpouring of the Holy Spirit upon the land of Scotland.

While it has to be conceded that Raymond did not see that revival in his day, yet who could deny the benefits accrued from such holy exercise. Young or inexperienced believers learned the difference between "saying prayers" and praying in the power of the Holy Spirit. The discipline of holding with determination to a fixed given objective was upheld, instead of the "World Tour" rambling prayers beloved of many. There is sharp contrast between the "vain repetition" which is the hallmark of many a church gathering, and the effectual fervency commended by Scripture. The apt "pupil" learned much in this "school of the prophets" which he would have been hard pressed to have experienced anywhere else.

Chapter 7

Raymond's Secular Labour

Raymond was a carpenter, or a joiner as the term is in Scotland. He worked in the heart of Clydeside for many years, mainly engaged in the repair of houses owned by the local authority. This allowed him to circulate primarily with working class people for whom he had special affection. Robert Liddle was a workmate of Raymond's for around thirteen years, and although not a professing evangelical Christian, yet he held Raymond in the very highest esteem. "I remember very well when I first met him in 1967," Robert said. "I knew him by sight because we were both employed by the Works Department of Clydebank Town Council, but it was 1967 before we came together in what was to be an exceptionally happy relationship."

It so happened that in 1968 there was a tremendous storm over the West of Scotland. One house in Vanguard Street, Clydebank, had lost half of its roof due to the gale force winds. Robert recalled one particular day when it was raining in a torrential deluge. Having been promised some assistance to repair the roof as quickly as possible in the atrocious conditions, he was eagerly awaiting this help, while trying to make some repair to the badly damaged roof himself.

Raymond was the promised assistance, and when he arrived, he and Robert, climbed the ladder to the roof and commenced further work together in the howling wind and downpour, though soaked to the skin. Conscious of the need of the family whose roof was badly leaking, they laboured on, working furiously until they were peering through drenching rain and seeking, by the illumination of the street lights, to try and make the roof watertight. Robert said, "The last nail was finally hammered home and we turned wearied, sodden, but grateful to descend the ladder. Such was the extensive damage that the gales had caused, that the equipment was not sufficient to meet all the emergencies that ensued, and unknown to the weary pair, someone had come and taken the ladder away for another emergency. Instead of coming off the roof at five o'clock, they had to suffer the storm and continual soaking until around 9.30 in the winter evening. Somebody suddenly remembered their plight and came to rescue them. "That," said Robert, "was how I spent my first day with Raymond McKeown! But, though we had such a miserable start to our friendship, the next twelve years were the happiest years that I ever experienced working with any mate."

Now Raymond had the respect of the other workers, though none shared his evangelical views. His beliefs never hampered his ability to integrate socially with his fellow workers, but without compromising his stand in the Gospel. Robert, in his own words, made the telling observation that, "Raymond's religion never dampened the spirits of anyone, but brightened the lives of people. This was what the men liked about his religious views. Now when Raymond came into the company of people they immediately felt at ease because of his wonderful attitude." Robert continued, "There wasn't a man on the workforce that did not have the greatest respect for Raymond. I used to be in the workshop first in the morning and when he would come in about ten minutes before starting time, if there was some music on the old battered radio we kept there, Raymond was off. He would grab me and whirl me around and dance to an old-time waltz while the others looked on in amazement. They could not understand how anyone could be so happy before commencing another day's drudgery, especially on cold winter mornings." Humorous or foolish as it may have appeared, yet it impressed hard bitten tough Clydeside workers as to the reality of the joy that Raymond's religion brought to his living.

Around 1967 the last of the great ocean liners, the Queen Elizabeth II, was launched in the old John Brown's shipyard. This was the end of an era which had included the building of the mighty Cunard Line giants, the Queen Mary and the Queen Elizabeth. Things would never be the same again on Clydeside and shipbuilding would gradually expire under unrelenting pressure from the industrious and ingenious Orientals. However, it would not expire without a fight and this battle was led by another Clydesider of different persuasion, a character called Jimmy Reid. Jimmy was the leading figure and spokesman for the famous or infamous — depending on your political viewpoint — workers' "sit-in" at the former John Brown's shipyard. He became a media personality with his articulate defence of the "right to work" philosophy which he and other Trade Union officials espoused. As a shop steward, the British term for labour representative, he occasionally came in contact with Raymond. Politically, as a Communist, Jimmy Reid was much further left than Raymond ever was, but they both had gifts of oratory and special skills in their own fields.

Raymond succeeded his mate and friend Robert Liddle as shop steward for the Works Department in Clydebank, "Because," Robert said, "he hated injustice of any kind. He didn't take the position, as many did for the sake of wielding authority, but because of a genuine interest in the welfare of his fellow workers. He never used the position to further his own ends or advance his own ambitious schemes. Jimmy Reid and his trade union colleagues led the workers to physically take over the shipyard when threatened with closure, and they continued a lengthy, but finally unsuccessful, attempt to run the yard themselves. In the process, however, they became media figures, especially Reid, and newspapers and television programmes featured him regularly, pontificating on matters which eventually went far beyond the realms of Trade Unionism or political affairs.

It was when Jimmy Reid was perhaps engulfed and swept away somewhat with the euphoria that certain sectors of public opinion generated for a time, that he engaged in some discussion with Raymond. Maybe the fact that Jimmy was very well versed in areas like sport and music, as well as politics, deluded him into thinking that no subject was beyond his competent appraisal. But, he palpably demonstrated at times in some of his media statements, a lamentable ignorance in religious matters. For example, an inability to distinguish the practical difference between a hyper-Calvinist and a biblically reformed believer, or indeed a true believer and a mere religious person. In fairness, it would have to be conceded that many professing Christians are also deficient in making this distinction. Discussing Burns' poem, "Holy Willie's Prayer," on a radio broadcast, Reid demonstrated his lack of knowledge on this point, although he spoke in most authoritive tone regarding his interpretation of the work. Such ignorance can perhaps go unchallenged in the arena of the untutored, and be acceptable in the superficiality of unlearned debate, but not when in engaged in discussion with one theologically equipped like Raymond undoubtedly was. Raymond recalled one interesting discussion as follows:

Jimmy Reid and another couple of Communist councillors had taken part in an ecumenical gathering which had been reported in the Press under the heading, "Protestants, Catholics and Communists worship together." Raymond had met Jimmy Reid around this time at a shop stewards' meeting. Jimmy stated during discussion that he "considered the Sermon on the Mount to be the greatest moral or ethical statement in the world." Raymond said that he was gratified to hear this and then remarked, "If you have such a high regard for that sermon and its author, then what is your opinion of this statement which he made on a crucially important issue? In the third chapter of John's Gospel, the one you have such high regard for, He also said, 'Verily, verily, I say unto thee. Except a man be born again he cannot see the Kingdom of God." Jimmy Reid at this juncture abruptly closed the conversation, perhaps realising that he was unable to counter the logic which Raymond presented.

Jimmy Reid, as an emerging celebrity, was invited to engage in a varied range of public debates covering a diversity of subjects like politics, sport and religion. It is a tragic fact that those generally enlisted by the media to defend the biblical Christian position are often sadly deficient even in the fundamentals of the matter. Christians are not beyond reproach in this contest either and often display a short sighted sectarian attitude in their choice of masters of polemic. One outstanding example of an evangelical who could have matched the prowess of Reid and un-horsed his arguments was Raymond McKeown. The evangelical church is often more concerned with a party spirit and partisan support of their own favourite idols, than of a proper defence of the truth by the most able exponents.

The ecumenical farce was all the motivation that Raymond required to take up the pen. In a letter to a local newspaper, his incisive wit and biting sarcasm were harnessed to expose the cant and hypocrisy and illogical unholy alliance formed by the participating parties. The letter is reproduced here:

> Sir,
> Baillie Henderson has delivered himself of a homily on the aims, objects and sundry employments of the Communist Party group within Clydebank Town Council, for which we are dutifully thankful.
> We must confess, however, to being mystified as to what role

the trio plan to fill in the spiritual life of the community.

A recent headline in your paper, "Protestants, Cathlolics and Communists Worship Together," was the description given to a recent religious service in the Town Hall.

We can well understand Protestants and Catholics worshipping together. Since the former are a pale imitation of the followers of John Knox, and the latter have taken to courting them with a view to marriage — in a Roman Catholic chapel of course, for the Ne Temere Decree would forbid otherwise, ecumenical love duets notwithstanding.

The erstwhile "heretics" have now become "separated brethren" by as fine a bit of ecclesiastical jugglery as one could wish for.

But who, or what were the Communists worshipping? We did not have the opportunity to view at close quarters, so we wish to know if the doughty sons of the Glorious Revolution closed their eyes when the parson was holding a soliloquy with his own innards — which is what prayer becomes if atheism be true.

Did they slip a hard earned shilling, earned as proletariat wage slaves, into the coffers of the enemy of the workers when the offering came round?

Did they lend a lusty Bolshevik baritone to the rendering of a "Mighty Fortress is Our God" (sung with a small "g" presumably?).

Religion — as Marx said, and his followers have parrotted ever since — "is the opium of the people." We wonder if, when having a puff at the pipe of peace at the Town Hall religious service, the opium had gone to their heads and they were becoming addicts.

Who knows what will become of us all if this state of affairs continues?

Perhaps a May Day procession in Moscow, led by the Rising Sons of William Flute Band, with the Ancient Order of Hibernians bringing up the rear, and the Clydebank brigade of the Party singing, while wedged between the tanks and rockets and other emblems of peace, a jolly ditty composed equal parts of the "Sash," "Faith of Our Fathers" and the "Red Flag."

You never know nowadays, do you?"

Robert Liddle could say of his workmate Raymond, what Willie Docherty had said in essence some years previously regarding his co-worker in the Gospel. "Working with Raymond was the happiest experience of my life, and my life was the better for the experience." It is quite remarkable that the same testimony should come from both spiritual and secular sources. Robert continued, "I spent several years in the army, met hundreds of men there, I worked all my life in the building trade and met hundreds of men there also, but I only ever met one Raymond! You've got to work with a man to know him, and every day for over twelve years I loved to work with Raymond. Mind you, he had the worst tools I ever saw a tradesman possess. The saws were old and blunt, the chisels, ancient with chipped blades. The planes and screwdrivers were likewise in a sorry state." It has to be recorded, however, that Raymond had done a lot of jobbing repair work for Factors of old property, and this caused considerable wear and tear on tools.

The undoubted love and respect that Robert Liddle had for his workmate should be kept in mind when reading his account of a humorous incident, which otherwise might have been thought offensive: "Raymond got a bit depressed. What, with all the trade union business and his religious activities, it wasn't surprising. I used to get a wee bit discouraged myself, and one day he would cheer me up, and another day I would cheer him up. Well, this particular day I was feeling a bit down and Raymond said to me, 'Never mind Robert. Just remember that the Lord Jesus was a carpenter just like you and me.' Aye, that's right Raymond, so he was, and when he died he must have left you his tools."

The compassion Raymond had for his fellow men is well demonstrated in this narrative, which was typical of many incidents in his daily routine. "We went to do a job for a lady in a local council house," Robert recalled, "And on a previous visit we had discovered that her husband was lying seriously ill in the bedroom suffering from a brain tumour. We asked the lady how her husband was, and she said that he was now in the Southern General Hospital in a critical condition. Now when anyone told Raymond anything of this nature, he was extremely sympathetic and understanding. The lady was making us a cup of tea around three o'clock that afternoon, when the telephone rang in the adjoining room. On answering the phone she suddenly let out a loud cry of anguish and we both rushed through to the next room. 'My husband is dead!' she gasped as she replaced the receiver. 'I've got to get over to the hospital right away'."

The Southern General Hospital is located south of the River Clyde from Clydebank where she lived. Although only a few miles away, yet without owning a car and having to travel by public transport, it was a most awkward place to reach. Without hesitation Raymond said, "Robert, will you finish the job here, and I'll get the lady over to the hospital immediately?" "Look, Raymond. I knew you were going to say that the moment this happened, so just you carry on and I'll finish the work here and wait for you to get back." Robert continued, "Well, off they went, and I washed up the tea cups and set them out on the table for their return. It was about six-thirty when they came back, so we had another cup of tea and sat and talked with the lady and consoled her for a while before we went home. First thing next morning, Raymond was back down at the house and again took the woman over to the hospital to collect the death certificate. Now, I had met her before, but Raymond had not, yet out of sheer goodness of his heart he was willing to do everything in his power to help a person in distress."

The continual outflow of good deeds from Raymond's life, though prolific, were but a peripheral part of the massive contribution he made individually for the maintenance and extension of the Kingdom of God. At this period, in the early Seventies, his open air work was prodigious and thousands heard the Gospel every week at the shipyard gates and factory sites. The unceasing warfare against the pornography trade also demanded much of his time. Letters continued to flow from his pen to all areas of the media. The Christian public had an "ostrich attitude" to much of the erosion of moral values around this time and articles even appeared in Christian periodicals which were critical of the kind of action and stand those of Raymond's persuasion adopted. This is an extract from a letter in 1971 in response to an article in the "Life of Faith:"

"Is it the Christian's place to protest against these abominations? Ask Wilberforce, ask Shaftesbury, ask Elizabeth Fry, ask John Howard, ask W. T. Snead, ask Bramwell Booth, ask Livingstone. These godly people, fired with a holy and righteous indignation, raised their voices against exploitation, slavery, brutality, and some even suffered imprisonment unjustly to awaken the slumbering conscience of the church regarding outrages against morality and decency which the smug and complacent ignore.

In these matters I believe it is my Christian duty to kneel and march; to pray and protest; to love and to legislate." Having taken a public stand on the issue, I find that my workmates and un-saved friends are not alienated by my position, but

comment that it is the sort of thing a Christian should do. They
expect me to oppose un-cleanness tooth and nail.''

Raymond McKeown.

The talents and gifts that Raymond possessed were not entirely
overlooked by his contemporaries and he was sought for several
evangelical positions in the midst of all his multi-faceted labours.
The Templemore Hall Assembly in Belfast had already approached
him originally in 1965 and still entertained hope of his consenting
to their requests for him to become pastor of the church. An eighteen
month spell in the Mount Merrion Free Presbyterian Church in
Belfast commenced around 1962, but, for various reasons, did not
prove a fruitful time in Raymond's ministry. This first experience
of being a full-time minister, and the legitimate demands of a
congregation caused Raymond much anxiety. Divergence of views
over the priorities in the church ministry and the added burden of
the McKeown children who never really settled in Belfast,
precipitated an early return to the more familiar scenes of the West
of Scotland. Many years were to pass before Raymond would
respond to a call to a ministerial office in any church.

On his return to the familiar heath, Raymond threw himself into
the various aspects of his Christian service with renewed vigour. His
open air training and pedigree were impeccable and, in the course
of open air work, he came in contact with some well-known figures
in the evangelical world. This never proved any difficulty for
Raymond, because he was as expert as a chairman at a meeting as
he was in taking the preaching responsibility himself. A winsome,
effervescent, humorous, but dignified presentation, won over the
listeners. Ever apt and relevant in his introductions, he made it easy
for any preacher to participate in the meeting and he always handed
over the "pulpit" as it were, having created a good atmosphere and
real sense of the presence of God.

One leading figure Raymond met was James A. Stewart, a native
Glaswegian, who, as a youngster of fourteen, began evangelising in
his own city before ministering throughout Britain, where he was
known as the "Boy Preacher." Before the second World War he
was led by God to carry the Gospel, especially in what are now termed
"Eastern Bloc" countries. He saw mighty moves of the Spirit in
places like Latvia, Estonia, Poland, Czechoslovakia, Hungary and
Bulgaria. Raymond introduced him at the famous Glasgow Cross

meeting one Sunday afternoon in the early Sixties. Having long been a resident of the United States, it was a nostalgic moment for James Stewart to preach again in the once familiar streets of his own home town.

It is perhaps not generally known that Raymond also led a meeting in Clydebank for an even more famous figure in 1955. It was the time of the great Billy Graham campaign in the Kelvin Hall in Glasgow. For six weeks the people flocked to the gatherings from all over Scotland in their thousands. Part of the preliminaries and peripheral activities included some open air meetings around Clydeside. Harry Gilpin recalled this particular time and described it in his own words like this:

"Ray and I were detailed by the Open Air Mission to cover the Billy Graham campaign in the Kelvin Hall in Glasgow. This was a tremendous opportunity because the posters were everywhere and the whole city was stirred up about this visit by Billy Graham. There was saturation advertising and we decided to cash in on this opportunity. We organised open air meetings at various factory and shipyard gates and went to the Billy Graham Crusade office to ask for any member of the team who was available, to come and speak for us. They all came including Billy himself. One of the greatest open air meetings we ever had was at the gates of John Brown's shipyard in Clydebank. We provided the Gospel caravan and Billy used this to address hundreds of workers who gathered during their lunch hour. George Beverley Shea sang, Cliff Barrows led the hymns and God just seemed to hover over the meeting as hundreds of men who probably seldom went to church, listened to the Gospel."

Three years later Billy Graham was back for "follow-up" meetings in Glasgow and once again Raymond contacted him regarding participation in some open air meetings. The times were changing and neither the euphoria or interest of 1955 was repeated in 1958. However, part of the preliminaries and peripheral activities again included open air meetings. One of these, organised by Raymond for shipyard workers and inhabitants of a working-class area in Dumbarton Road, Clydebank, was just adjacent to John Brown's shipyard.

The situation was vastly different to what Billy Graham was used to, because the venue was no massive arena or sports stadium, but what is commonly known as a "back court" in the West of Scotland. This was the back area, usually tarred, of the grey or red sandstone tenement buildings which lined most main roads at this time. They normally had old brick washing houses and clothes poles for hanging up the washing to dry. They were dismal places at the best of times, because they were usually in the shadow of the four storey tenement, and often backed on to a high factory wall.

Such was the site of the open air meeting where Raymond introduced Billy Graham to a very small Clydeside audience. Without the back-up of the usual arena, mass choirs, superb music, powerful public address system, Billy was exposed to the harsh reality of life as lived by the majority of Scots in their own surroundings. Raymond at home in the familiar scenario, with his battered accordion, tiny battery-operated microphone, quickly warmed to the task. He introduced the famous evangelist in his inimitable way and Billy Graham delivered a brief Gospel message to a few dozen people. It must truthfully be recorded that the message had little obvious impact, although the great evangelist preached as well as he could in the rather unfamiliar spartan conditions. Devoid of the support ministries, and the atmosphere of the mighty arena, he seemed vulnerable and mortal as other men. It would be true to say that whether in the midst of evangelical media personalities, or unique men of God in missionary or theological confines, the "master craftsman" was unsurpassed in his own peculiar and special ministry.

Raymond had an overwhelming desire to see the best in any person. His truly gregarious nature, magnanimity, and self-effacing way, continually manifested the spirit of the peace-maker within him. However, he had his own lines of demarcation and separation, which he genuinely and sadly felt he must implement at all times. The course of the Billy Graham Crusade ministry in the Sixties began to fill him with doubt and apprehension. Billy, by association and indentification with Modernists and Roman Catholics, began to alienate the conservative evangelicals of Raymond's persuasion. An unsatisfactory reply to a query he made to the Crusade organisation in Glasgow regarding where converts from Roman Catholic churches would be directed after their conversion reluctantly left him with no alternative than to withdraw his support from the Graham campaigns. He did this in his own quiet way and made no mention of it in public.

Raymond had great affection and sympathy with the Presbyterian cause, but although he had opportunities to enter its ministry and could have felt much at home there, he confided that: "I could never

71

become a Presbyterian because I cannot entertain the doctrine of infant baptism.''

A sensitive conscience and practical resolution to stand for what he held dear, were qualities of integrity which have become scarcer in the superficial days in which we now live. He would not perjure his conscience for the advancement of natural desire or ambition and yet retained a wide circle of evangelical friends of all persuasions. This probably resulted from an oft quoted philosophy of his that, ''We must always separate the man from his message or doctrine.'' In his antagonism to the Roman Catholic system, he loved Roman Catholic sinners. His attitude to Christians of differing beliefs was of like nature.

Chapter 8

Warfare Against Pornography

1960 was the year that Princess Margaret married photographer Antony Armstrong-Jones in Westminster Abbey. Sixteen years later they would be divorced, confirming that even the Royal Family were not immune from the rapidly accelerating moral decline that was overtaking the nation. Natural disasters also took place in this decade of the Sixties and the Aberfan mining village, south of Merthyr Tydfil in Wales, claimed 144 dead, most of them children, when a mountain of black slag engulfed houses and the local school. Not only moral pollution affected the country, but the oil tanker Torrey Canyon ran aground near the Scilly Isles, and in breaking apart, discharged over 100,000 tons of crude oil on the coasts of Cornwall and Devon. The Beatles were given MBE's by the Queen, much to the consternation of many solid citizens. The Conservative politician Enoch Powell was warning that the immigration policy would cause riot and violence in the big cities. Bishop John Robinson made headlines with his book, "Honest to God," which attacked the traditional concept of the deity of Christ. It was against this background that Raymond laboured almost single handed, in combat against the architects and vendors of moral pollution, who distributed pornographic literature, and films.

Queen Street railway station, situated on George Square, the focal point of the city of Glasgow, is one of the stations which survived the great decline in railway traffic since the Second World War. It serves the northern part of Scotland primarily, and is a busy commuting centre, as well as having many long distance trains in its daily busy schedule.

It was a rather miserable wet Saturday evening when Raymond strolled down Dundas Street on the West side of the railway terminal. Access can be gained to the station from this entrance and Raymond was particularly interested in this entry. Not for the first time had he made this trip with a particular purpose in view. He mingled with a collection of travellers making their way home, and shoppers, football fans and an occasional hiker or mountaineer braving the vagaries of a Scottish winter evening to "get away from it all" and enjoy the lure of the hills and lochs in spite of an inhospitable climate. Merging with the throng, Raymond was just another traveller being carried along with the human tide that converged and funnelled through the entrance to the various platforms.

A seemingly innocuous newspaper vendor, plied his wares right at the entry. Legally he was supposed to be in Dundas Street, outwith railway property, but a chill Scottish winter night and the hurrying muffled crowds scarcely noticed the huddled figure with his newspapers and magazines spread out on the pavement and station entrance. The vendor's family had occupied the site for over three generations, and, it was not in Raymond's mind to deprive honest working folks of their living. However, in the changing moral climate that spanned the time scale from the old steam locomotives to the new modern diesel units, the filth of moral degradation had invaded to some extent the lives of all the population.

Raymond paused in the station entrance, an inconspicuous onlooker in the anonymous garb of an ordinary Glasgow working-class citizen. His eyes quickly scanned the display of newspapers and magazines set out on the pavement and arranged right into the entrance doorway itself. In the gloom of the wet September evening, it was hard to see clearly by the artificial lighting supplied mainly by the street lamps, but he soon located the objects of his intent. Situated at the back of the displayed material were the offending items. Commonly known as "girlie" magazines, their lurid covers showed various nude or scantily clad girls in flagrantly sexual poses. Raymond, being well versed in the necessities of the law in regard to complaints about pornographic literature, knew that he had to purchase a copy of the offending publication and specifically detail the text or photographs he considered obscene and offensive. Always able to see the funny side of the most depressing or offending situations, he wondered that some of the "holier than thou" brigade of Christians might think if they came upon him at the precise moment he purchased the obscene publication.

The next task was to compose a letter of complaint to the station manager concerning the use of railway property to sell pornographic literature. In 1971 he wrote to British Railways Scottish Region at

Queen Street Station and received the following rather inconclusive reply.

Dear Sir,

Thank you for your letter of 8th September, 1971, and I can assure you that no trader of any description has received Railway Board permission to sell offensive literature on railway premises.

After your previous complaints, Police observations over a period have not found the vendor to be in possession of any literature which would be classed as obscene, and consequently there was no further action the Police could take regarding this matter.

Whilst I may personally sympathise with your viewpoint, in my opinion, the real issue you raise is a general one and not a specific one. What constitutes obscene literature is determined by the law, and I can only take official action within the terms of the law. As you probably know, similar literature to that to which you refer, is sold and displayed by most reputable booksellers.

I have however made a personal approach to the newsvendor concerned, and he has told me that rather than cause serious trouble, he would cease dealing in these magazines.

Yours faithfully,

Station Manager.

Less dedicated or determined campaigners might have settled for that reply. Although inferring that the police had found nothing objectionable in their regular scrutiny of the site, and expressing a personally sympathetic support, in addition to having the word of the worthy vendor that he would no longer offer the offending material for sale, Raymond was still unimpressed. Having a perceptive understanding of the vagaries of human nature, he suspected that the matter was as yet far from successfully concluded. So he pressed on with his complaint. It has to be borne in mind that Raymond was quite often conducting several campaigns of this nature concurrently, as well as continuing all his other activity in the Gospel.

When Raymond got "the bit between his teeth" he took a lot of stopping. This incident was typical of his rugged determination when he felt strongly about an issue. Various letters proceeded from his pen to the police, magistrates and the British Rail Board. A year later this particular battle was successfully concluded as the following letter from the Procurator-Fiscal's department clearly shows. Writing to one of the City Councillors whom Raymond had petitioned with regard to the matter, the Procurator-Fiscal wrote:

Dear Sir,

Further to my letter of 28th March, I have to report that, following investigation by the police, a warrant was obtained, under which the stance in Dundas Street was raided and the vendor charged with keeping for sale 781 indecent or obscene books, papers, etc., in contravention of Section 162 or the 1960 Act. The relative police information has been duly marked for prosecution by summons. The 781 books, etc., were seized as productions.

Yours sincerely,

Procurator Fiscal of Police.

Through the Sixties and Seventies the tidal wave of moral pollution engulfed the nation. Raymond had scant encouragement from the majority of his fellow Christians in the war against the great decline of wholesome biblical standards. They had no stomach for the physical effort and mental stress which such activity induced. On a national level, a former art mistress, Mary Whitehouse, developed into a formidable campaigner in association with the Festival of Light, and this was an encouragement to such activists as Raymond. But, evil men, the terrible declension of religious interest, and increasing apathy among Christian people, regarding the great social and moral questions of the day, did little to encourage Raymond in his mainly single-handed fight against the irresistable tide of permissiveness which characterised this period of history.

A sinister and wicked development of the pornographic literature scourge was the spawning of sex shops and sexually explicit video tapes. With censorship abolished, the theatre was able to stage shows like "Oh Calcutta" where nudity was displayed without reservation. This and factors like the ever increasing use of nude photographs in daily newspapers provided the impetus and conditioned the public for the introduction of sex shops or "Private Shop" as they were called.

The first attempt to introduce such an establishment was made in Glasgow near St. George's Cross on Great Western Road. Amid the inevitable media publicity, an erstwhile drain cleaning services owner seemed anxious of the dubious honour of being the first sex shop proprietor in Scotland. This impending blot on the face of his native city incensed Raymond and immediate plans were activated to counter this proposal. The shop, which was sited opposite the old Underground station, duly opened with a somewhat shamefaced owner seeking to defend his motive of providing a needed service for a neglected section of the populace.

On the first Saturday after the opening, the pickets were outside the shop in force. Any potential customer had to run the gauntlet of the placards of the Christians and the jeers of the onlookers. Raymond, in conjunction with some other Christian friends, had organised a march of protest which would commence in the city centre and finally arrive at the doorstep of the sex shop. Around 700 protesters gathered on a pleasant sunny day, festooned with banners and placards and led by some musicians. They marched and sang their way through the city to arrive en masse outside the sex shop. A brief service was held and prayer made for the removal of this scourge in the city. Extensive television and media coverage was given and the campaign heralded the fairly rapid demise of the first ''Private Shop.''

The merchants and vendors of sin are not, however, easily dissuaded from their evil business, and later, in the Seventies, Raymond was confronted with the advent of another sex shop in his own locality. The proprietors of this establishment had a nationwide chain and were not to be discouraged so easily as the first ''porno-pest!'' Local residents were marshalled and with church leaders of differing persuasions, a new assault against the might of a London based organisation was planned. Raymond had no indication initially of the iniquitous depths to which these protagonists would stoop.

Dumbarton Road is the main street of the old established Partick area, in the west of the city. It is a working-class district primarily, with quite a colony of Highland folks, who generally are of a pious disposition. It was here that Raymond and Violet had lived most of their married life and raised their family. It was here that Raymond had wrestled with the intricacies of theology and forged a genuine irrevocable conviction as to the authenticity of the reformed doctrines of grace. Implicit in such belief was the fact of the total depravity of man. As a consequence of the Fall in Adam, man was corrupt and depraved from the soles of his feet to the crown of his head. In the Christian pilgrimage and warfare, God sees fit, in His own divine appointment, to test the validity and integrity of His servants. Theoretical convictions which melt before the challenge of adversity,

77

or capitulate to the blandishment of personal advancement or commendation of men, are merely manifested as disposable opinions. To survive the rigours or spiritual warfare, this is the acid test! The McKeown family were about to be put to the test on the basis of this principle in a dastardly and devilishly vile way.

It was a mark of the aggravation which the "porn" merchants or their supporters felt that they devised a plot of fiendish wickedness to vent their spleen against those who opposed their filthy operation. The Press had reported that £10,000 of stock from the sex shop had been confiscated on the day prior to opening. The three men who worked in the premises were taken to the police station and charged with intention to sell indecent, profane and obscene articles. Although it was never legally established who instigated the offences against the leading figures in the anti-pornography battle, few people were in doubt who the culprits were.

The "Private Shops" distributed a magazine which catered for the perverted tastes of the type of clientele they attracted. A bogus advertisement was inserted in this sick publication listing the telephone numbers of leading protesters and inviting enquiry for participation in all manner of lewd and obscene practices. The McKeowns began to receive these vile phone calls after the advert stated that, "a mother and daughter were available for group sex." Any normal decent person can imagine the shock and revulsion which such phone calls produced and the nervous tension generated by the simple everyday experience of the telephone ringing. Raymond and Violet displayed remarkable resilience and cheerfulness in the very distressing circumstances. Every opportunity was taken to witness for Christ to the callers and many of them retired from their initial perverted approach, disconcerted, to say the least.

The degrading episode was brought to the attention of the police and Raymond wrote various letters, even to the Prime Minister, Mrs. Thatcher. The proprietors withdrew the magazines from 130 branches throughout the country just as a "hornets' nest" of protest from many quarters arose. Raymond received a letter from Mrs. Thatcher's office as follows:

> Dear Mr. McKeown,
> The Prime Minister has asked me to thank you for your letter of 12th November, concerning the placing of bogus advertisements containing your name and address and telephone

number in a "sex magazine" and the unfortunate repercussions which have ensued. Mrs. Thatcher fully sympathises with the distress that this has caused you and your family.

In the midst of the trauma which such a situation would produce, Raymond had to contend with the smug comments which were sometimes delivered by contributors to the Christian Press. Generally written by those who were completely out of touch with the practicalities of living at grass roots level, there was a flippancy and irresponsibility about their attitude which must have incensed those servants of God seeking to take a stand against the "emporiums of filth," as Raymond described them. To be subjected to the wickedness and abuse that the protesters endured and to suffer the ultimate indignity of uninformed criticism from fellow Christians, seemed hard to bear. This excerpt from a reply Raymond made to such negative criticism reveals something of the hurt and indignation that such scribes induced by their banal comments.

> "Does your contributor realise for one moment the matters about which we protest? Does he seriously imagine that sane people would parade the streets complaining of such trivia as the distance from the pavement of a skirt hem or the peculiar use to which Holman Hunt put the face of his mistress for artistic purposes? I would suggest that such naivety debars a man from passing public comment and criticism on his fellow Christians.

> As a parent I have a responsibility to my family to do all I can to be as salt to the world's corruption. As a Christian, I am my brother's keeper, and responsible to God for him. In both these aspects I am convinced it is my solemn duty to protest against corruption and filth."

Does protest accomplish anything? This question invariably arose and though it was sometimes asked as a genuine query, more often than not it was posed as a justification for inactivity or lack of concern for current moral issues. That it was a dirty business with a capability to pollute and degrade is unquestionable. That it required a special type of individual to engage in such warfare may be fair comment. But nevertheless, general apathy and indifference among the Christian community was commonplace. Doubtless, Raymond was uniquely equipped to handle the distressing and degrading situations that were inevitably encountered in the prosecution of such protest. To have to handle the pornographic material was in itself a contaminating and polluting experience, but Raymond had that detached aplomb which seemed to allow him contact with, and exposure to, the vilest merchandise while remaining apparently unscathed.

In material and moral terms, it must be recorded that Raymond's efforts with the small band of occasional helpers, achieved a considerable degree of success in both these realms. In material terms, many thousands of pounds worth of obscene literature and objects were confiscated and destroyed. This hit the porno vendors where it hurt. The fact of the eventual closing down of the "Private Shop" in Partick, and the general harassment of the premises whilst they remained open, surely restricted the flow of filth to the community at large. The ability to maintain the prodigious work rate that characterised Raymond's life at this time, was obviously a gift of God. During the most stressful and distressing periods of this decade, there was absolutely no diminishing of the output of spiritual activity in the Gospel, either in relation to the unconverted or the people of God. Only a regular and perceptive observer would have detected the signs of strain or depression which occasionally manifested when his guard was relaxed in the presence of close personal friends.

One example of the other activities that Raymond managed to cram into his busy life during this period was to accept an invitation to speak in Stirling University at a festival entitled, "Christ and Modern Man." The seminar included an impressive list of speakers, mostly with doctorates and various degrees. Raymond was invited to speak on "Biblical Thought and Trade Unionism." The festival's objective was to present a biblical view of all areas of contemporary life, and Raymond, without the benefit of a formal education, was nevertheless adequately equipped to function, even in the rarefied strata of academic excellence.

Another facet of Raymond's ministry was directed toward the cinema queues which proliferated in Glasgow before the advent of television caused a decline in this form of entertainment. It was a rather boring exercise to stand in line for perhaps an hour or so in Sauchiehall Street, awaiting admission to the cinema, and so any diversion was welcomed. It took the most inclement weather to deter Raymond and his band of helpers from adjoining themselves to a convenient queue and spending a brief twenty minutes or so in bringing the Gospel message to many who never entered the precincts of any place of worship. Standing at the edge of the pavement, the trusty old accordion strapped around his back, Raymond would lead off in one of the popular hymns or choruses such as "I'm Following Jesus." Then, with a few apt and humorous remarks, he soon had the crowd's attention. There is no doubt that before he had finished, many of them had momentarily forgotten the reason why they were standing in line. So the Gospel was continually propagated, out where the sinners were.

The Welfare State, though extensive in its coverage of the needs of the under-privileged, had still left a residue of the population with unresolved difficulties and problems in maintaining the essentials of living. Whether some of these suffer from their own foolishness or inability to cope with the stress of modern society is debatable, but the fact of their undoubted need remains. Raymond had a genuine concern for the downtrodden and derelicts of society and expressed this compassion in his great interest in the Tent Hall breakfasts. They were an institution in the life of evangelical Glasgow, and provided sustenance for body and soul in the "down and out" community for many years.

Around 1967 commenced his interest in the free breakfast work and maintained this until the cessation of the work in the Eighties. At the height of the popularity of the free breakfast, a tea urn capable of supplying 8,000 cups was in use. 1877 was the year of the opening of the Tent Hall and 2,000 people were not uncommon at the free breakfast in those days.

Raymond rose early on a Sunday morning in April, 1970. It was about 6.15 a.m. and he had a quick cup of tea before hurrying downstairs and crossing over Dumbarton Road to await one of the members of the open air team who had arranged to give him a lift and go to the free breakfast that morning. There was not much stir at this early hour on a Sunday morning, and Raymond contemplated the early morning sun that was just giving hint of appearing over the rooftops of Patrick. "Looks like a decent day for the open air this afternoon," he mused, and the anticipation of this warmed him as he saw the car approaching, driven by Bob, one of the musicians who was going to assist at the very informal service that would accompany the free breakfast.

It did not take long to drive along Dumbarton Road and on through Argyle Street, before making a right turn down Saltmarket to the corner of Steel Street. Turning left into Steel Street, Raymond noted that they were in plenty of time for the prayer meeting that preceded the breakfast. From 7 a.m. till 7.30 a.m. the Christians would pray and seek God's blessing on the labours of the day. A considerable crowd of around a hundred or so regulars had already gathered, and some of them greeted Raymond with a variety of comments as he made his way into the Tent. After the prayer meeting, George Dunnet and one of the other workers would go to the door and then allow the crowd to file into the hall. Each one was greeted with a handshake and given a bag of food which generally consisted of items such as, two bread rolls with cheese, a meat pie, a pint mug for tea and a hymn sheet. It was an interesting but sad fact, that on numerous occasions some of the regular attenders were recovered by the police, drowned in the River Clyde and the only means of identification was a Tent Hall hymn sheet found in their pockets.

Bob Christie, now a television news reader, was the organist and pianist in the Tent, and around 8 a.m. he sat at the grand piano to play the opening psalm. Having filed into the main auditorium the assembled recipients, after singing the first psalm and awaiting a prayer of thanks for the provision of the food, were then served with tea and commenced to eat breakfast. Although this service was primarily organised for "down and outs," it was not unknown for a few thrifty Scots to mingle with the crowd and avail themselves of a free breakfast. This was also the only church service that the majority ever attended, so opportunity was taken to present the Gospel as well as provide the food.

Having eaten the food, some of the "worthies" had all means of containers available for acquiring sufficient tea for the remainder of the day. One bright spark produced an old rubber hot water bottle and proferred this for replenishing, which indicated an ingenious, if not hygenic turn of mind! Empty whisky bottles were also invariably produced. It was a unique cameo of life which reflected the tragedies of the misfits of society, some of whom were the product of their own folly, others of man's inhumanity to man. In spite of all the help and compassion shown to them, some of the attenders could, when denied, for example, an extra bag of food when supplies ran out, rant and rave with the foulest language. When the oaths and cursing were accompanied by statements like, "I've been coming here for forty years and you've given him the last bag of extra food," it was a tragic manifestation of the hardness of the impenitent heart against the continual entreaty of the Gospel appeal. Against this depressing statistic there were also the encouraging accounts of those who had responded to the message and included in the ranks of such were professional people, doctors and lawyers who had been gripped by the scourge of alcohol and had come to a knowledge of Christ and return to sanity through the ministry at the free breakfast. And insanity it surely was which could drive a man to drink hair lacquer or methylated spirit, with the inevitable irrepairable damage to health and lifespan which these habits induced.

The ladies and other helpers were clearing away and collecting the tea mugs in the hall, when Raymond, in familiar pose, came on to the platform adjusting the straps of the old faithful accordion. A few introductory remarks against the quietly played opening bars of "Amazing Grace" and then into the first verse of this ever-popular hymn of John Newton. The smiles of contentment which are readily produced from a satisfied stomach and the recognition of a well known melody, spread over the faces of many of the congregation. Faces lined and gnarled with years of sinning against conscience and against God. Grimy and careworn, displaying the ravages of rough living and insufficient diet. Eyes devoid of the sparkle or animation that says something of the inner life of a man. But Raymond loved them and they knew it. Cracked voices, tuneless voices, and some that had once had a degree of musicality, they joined together in singing the familiar well loved strain.

Raymond unstrapped the accordion and, surveying the motley crew which comprised his audience, he said, "Jesus Christ one day stood face to face with a man called Nicodemus. And Jesus said to Nicodemus, 'Nicodemus, you must be born again. Nicodemus, you must be born again,' and that's the very heart of the gospel of Jesus Christ. That men and women not only need a new start, but that men and women need a new heart. Now who was it that said you must be born again? The person who said, 'You must be born again, was the founder of the Christian church. It was Jesus Christ himself, and if man deny the necessity of the new birth they are saying that Jesus Christ is telling lies, when He says that men and women must be born again. Now if I come to this breakfast and tell you upon my own authority, that you must be born again, then there is ground for complaint, there is ground for discussion. But this word was spoken by the Lord Jesus Christ himself. Now we want you to get that plain, we want you to get that clear, this is not a message that originates in the heart of man. This is not a message that has been formed by the philosophy of man. This is the message of the founder of the Christian church!''

Raymond looked around at the collection of derlicts. Some had only been released from the police station that very morning, having been incarcerated after being found drunk and incapable in some city alley or back street. Many had battered, bruised faces that spoke eloquently and tragically of the rough justice of the twilight zone, their habitat, unknown to most of their fellow citizens. And as they looked at the ordinary unremarkable figure on the platform, they saw the man who had been buttering the rolls they had just eaten, and had been helping to fill the steaming mugs of tea. They mostly paid attention, through their befuddled minds sought constantly to orbit off on to some other track. Here was no aloof, cold cleric, no ecclesiastical dignitary, adorned with the paraphenalia that seems so loved by the effete clergy who mirror fallen man's concept of religious hierarchy. No, this was one of themselves, but more, what they might have been had they not chose the way of sin as opposed to the highway of holiness. In vain would they look for one of the gowned and collared figures from the established church coming to mingle where lice and filth, disease and smell, were the badge of the "down and out!" This man was a friend of sinners.

Raymond, knowing the capacity of most of the audience to listen was of short duration, and having simply expounded the famous verse from the third chapter of John's Gospel, began to wind up his address.

"Friends, Jesus spoke thus to Nicodemus, because Nicodemus was dead. But you say 'That's an impossibility, for Nicodemus was there. He was moving. He was talking. He was animate. He had all the marks of a man who was very much alive,' But Jesus, you see, wasn't talking about physical life. Jesus was talking about spiritual life. When he spoke about death, he was not speaking about a cessation of existence. Jesus was saying to Nicodemus that sin had separated him from the life that was in God, that men are born into the world sinners, that men are born into the world in a state of separation from God. Men are born in a state of being dead in iniquity! And when he said to Nicodemus, 'You must be born again,' He was saying that no man shall gain the Kingdom of Heaven unless he has a living vital relationship with the living God. Have you got it, friends? If you've never been born again of the Spirit of God, you're dead in your sins. If God by His Spirit and His blood has never cleansed you, you're dead in sin. You, by nature, are a child of wrath, for you are devoid of that quality of life that is suitable for heaven.''

By the Holy Spirit's enabling, Raymond had captivated the attention of most of those who had the capability to grasp simple facts. He had steadily increased the tempo and conviction so that he was now far removed from the apparently innocuous joking individual who had handed out the mugs of tea and buttered rolls.

About fifteen minutes had passed and Raymond drew to a conclusion, ''Now you may come and argue with us about this matter. You may say to us, 'I don't accept it.' Let me tell you what the Word of God says of men and women who reject that Word: 'He that believeth not hath made God a liar!' Have you got it? To call a man a liar is something, but to make a man a liar is something else. That's an offence, an outrage against his character. You refuse this Word of the living God to your soul this morning and you are making God a liar, you are libelling the character of God. I would not like to be in your shoes on the day of judgement. Jesus said to Nicodemus, 'You must be born again,' because Nicodemus was dead in trespasses and sin. Except you receive the risen life of Christ within that soul of yours, you shall remain dead and through all eternity you shall be separated from the life which is in God, separated from life in a place the Bible calls Hell. Whether we like it or not, that's what the Bible says. All right then, what will you now do with God's statement, 'You must be born again?''

There was no doubt that the needy souls in that Tent Hall free breakfast could not have had a more explicit and simple presentation of the truth and in this respect were more privileged than many who attended the gilded temples of nominal religion, or the citadels of weak ''easy believism'' which were beginning to supplant the truth in many places once covenanted to the old primitive evangel.

Another breakfast was over and Raymond mingled with the departing crowd. The usual busy Sunday events lay ahead and Raymond had some final conversation with some of the workers, on various Christian topics, before he set off for his many preaching engagements around the city. None captivated him more than the work of the free breakfast. Great Tent Hall Superintendents such as Peter Connoly, P. T. McRostie and Jock Troup had been associated with the free breakfast and it was a privilege to follow in their train.

As he watched some of the derelicts shuffling away to seek various means to acquire some money to buy drink of sufficient potency to obliterate the harsh reality of their lives, his mind pondered that defence mechanism which the natural man so often erected against the claims of Christ. He thought of his fellow workmates who often came to him at the work bench to confide, "It's all too much for me. I'm just going out for a drink." This was to blind themselves to the reality of being unable to cope with the pressures of life. "And yet," Raymond mused, "these are the fellows who would have nothing to do with the Gospel. They are the ones who run away from problems, deride Christians by saying, 'You Christians, you're running away from reality.' It's not us who run away from reality," Raymond thought. "It's these poor deluded souls who cannot face up to life, its difficulties and disappointments. But when a man comes face to face with the Lord Jesus, he comes face to face with final ultimate reality!"

With these thoughts passing through his mind, Raymond was out of Steel Street and had turned right up Saltmarket, making his way to Glasgow Cross where the open air meeting would take place later in the day. The seeds of a message for that gathering had already begun to germinate in his mind.

Chapter 9

A Man For His Generation

The Fifties and Sixties were the halcyon days of open air preaching in Britain during Raymond's lifetime. Wedded to what was almost an obsession for this work was an undiminishing compassion for the objects of the ministry. The average uninformed evangelical generally has a rather patronising attitude to the "street preacher," which conceded that he was a necessary adjunct to the Gospel ministry, but was usually carried on by those who were unfitted for a more orthodox ministry within the church. While this may be true in certain instances, it certainly did not apply in the case of the "master craftsman," Raymond McKeown. Raymond's spiritual lineage could be traced back to such as Howell Harris, the great Welsh exhorter, born in 1714. An exceedingly gifted man, Harris would probably have succeeded in any activity of life he had engaged in. Like him, Raymond was not an ordained clergyman, primarily because of the nature of his first love, open air preaching. Harris had the real "call of God" upon his life; so did Raymond. The sad malaise of the present generation, where young men, often unsuccessful in other areas of life, or with a higher estimation of their spiritual gifts and attainments than evidence warrants, launch themselves into the work of God, had no parallel in Raymond's call and ministry. What is perhaps more tragic is the fact that the generally spiritually unenlightened age in which we live encourages anyone who states that they "have a call" to make immediate application to Bible College, irrespective of any genuine evidence of real spiritual gifts. The thinking behind this often seems to be that there is some merit in having a "full-time worker" produced from the ranks. Doubtless where a genuine vessel has been raised up for unique ministry there might be some justification for such an assertion.

Harris, Wesley, Whitefield, were men raised for their generation and equipped by God beyond dispute. For Wesley to hold the attention of thousands at Gwennap pit, a great natural amphitheatre near Redruth in Cornwall, required strong convictions, extensive knowledge and gifted preaching ability. Wesley, like Harris and Whitefield, had the vital basic ingredients for successful ministry in any realm — a rock solid doctrinal basis and a sphere or field of labour suitable to their gifts and energies. Wesley doubtless possessed these attributes, but his doctrinal position, though securely fixed in his thinking, was not one with which George Whitefield could have sympathy. Raymond was of Whitefield's persuasion doctrinally, and his strong grip of the reformed doctrines of grace, commonly called Calvinism, was no secret. It is something of an uncommon quality, particularly in these days, that a strong believer in the sovereignty of God as Raymond was, should also have a burning evangelical heart for reaching sinners wherever they could be found.

Of all the great men of Calvinistic persuasion, Raymond's favourite was C. H. Spurgeon, who in his volume "Lectures To My Students," did much to counter the mischief wrought by some Bible Colleges in training men for the ministry. Easy going, friendly, natural personalities have often been moulded into distant, ministerial, haughty figures, who grant audiences in a most formal manner to the lower order of the species. Sometimes those handicapped by a surfeit of pride or unreality seem rather to have the malaise nurtured than destroyed. While it is true that a minister might have to guard his time against encroachment by the insensitive and perennial comfort seekers, yet it is a sad thing that many a cleric manifests a rigidly formal unreality in his dealings with the saints. To be friendly, informal and non-ministerial is seen as a great drawback with sections of the evangelical church, and indeed they seem rather to encourage than abhor the practice. A simple, down to earth approach is mistaken by many ministers as not being consistent with the dignity of the pastoral office. This attitude seems to be fostered in some colleges and denominations and appears to influence ministerial intoning, forms of gestures and an unreality which ought to have no place in the pulipts of the house of God. Spurgeon dealt admirably with this infection in the volume mentioned.

Raymond was totally real, and it would seem that those whom he greatly admired in the Christian ministry also had this characteristic to a greater or lesser degree. Perhaps a basic insecurity produces the need for visible separation and the maintenance of barriers which do not allow the preacher to descend to the level of the common man. At worst, it is a pathetic parody of the true role of the Christian minister, at best an obnoxious posture of unreality. Harris, Whitefield, Nettleton seemed possessed of a humility that enabled them to be readily available and be at the disposal of people in need, yet they did not apparently feel threatened by being "all things to all men."

Howell Harris, the Welshman, was a burning firebrand for God. The affinity that Raymond had with Harris was that neither were ordained clergymen, and both had a consuming passion for open air preaching, which God uniquely gifted them to exercise. Harris apparently did not possess the power of intellect that Raymond had, but on the other hand he shared a passion for the "secret place" which lent power and penetration to his ministry.

"In the secret place with God, Harris was in his element. That was his home — his chiefest pleasure. In Carmarthen at this time, when all the town went out to see the arrival of His Majesty's judges, Harris stole away to the secret place to pray.*

Harris, like the majority of those who espouse the doctrines of free grace, had begun his ministry with Arminian persuasions. His theological wanderings brought him to serious contemplation of his doctrinal views and the attitude of this contemporaries towards his view.

"The Churchmen of Breconshire were much pleased with this teaching. I hesitated when I understood that the carnally minded clergymen were pleased that I was calling Election the doctrine of the devil . . . When I denounced Election, many who formerly hated me began to love me for this reason. This led me to examine why they loved me; but yet I continued to proclaim that man could turn himself, as otherwise my preaching was vain."*

Harris continued to wrestle with the dilemma of these theological doubts until somewhat later he recorded, "Some time after this, whenever I opened the bible, my eyes seemed always to fall on John 6:44. But such was the enmity of my carnal reason against the wisdom of God, that I would secretly blame Infinite Wisdom for setting it there, and I strove diligently to explain away its real meaning. At last, the devil became my teacher, whispering to me, that God drew everybody. This served pretty well until I read verse 37 of the same chapter. Then I was brought to believe in Election in my heart; my

*"The early life of Howell Harris." Banner of Truth.

wisdom yielded to the wisdom of God, and I confessed with my mouth unto salvation."*

That attitude is still prevalent in evangelical circles today, but it was not one that found any favour with Raymond, although his beliefs in such truth had evolved and developed in his early years without the struggles that Harris endured.

Whitefield, perhaps the brightest star in the firmament of Calvinistic open air preachers, shared affinity with Raymond in his power of intellect, and in his humility of character, which was outstanding. This could be summarised in a statement Whitefield made to friends, when urged by them to reply to criticisms. He said, "I am content to wait till the judgement day for the clearing up of my character. When I am dead I desire no epitaph but this: 'Here lies George Whitefield. What kind of man he was the great day will discover'."

Raymond had known public attack and opposition, and once when most unjustly reviled from the pulpit publicly by a rather sensation seeking preacher, he adopted the same procedure as Whitefield and humbled himself under the hand of God so that He might vindicate or not, as He saw fit.

While there is no ultimate way to measure the comparative attributes in men, especially when their lives are separated by a long period of time, nevertheless Raymond shared various qualities and gifts with such men as Whitefield. Certainly in the realm of doctrine, Whitefield was able to develop his views through personal contact with such as the Erskine brothers and Harris. He also read extensively from such works as Boston's "Fourfold State of Man." Raymond had read these great works and much of the Puritan literature had matured his theological perspective also.

Raymond, unlike Whitefield and many others of strong religious conviction, never got into serious conflict regarding his doctrinal views, and while this may be admirable in the eyes of some, to others it was a weakness that he manifested. To hold firmly such great fundamental truths, yet subdue them so entirely that few of his fellow workers were ever really confronted with the implications of the doctrine or challenged regarding the validity of their own beliefs, says something for a true ecumenical spirit, but not so much perhaps for a desire to propagate truth to the less informed amongst the brethren. And it must be asserted that many with whom he

*"The Early Life of Howell Harris." Banner of Truth.

worked had a very limited doctrinal knowledge indeed.

As far as the Christian dialetic was concerned, Raymond adopted a very passive attitude. He was certainly not of the "prophet" mould, and it must be said that this probably accounted for some of the popularity that he enjoyed with the general Christian public. The role of peacemaker came naturally to him and he exercised this well, but even a peacemaker may have to "withstand to the face" on occasions when it is necessary to contend publicly against some doubtful Christian practice. or belief. Perhaps the only exception to this attitude came if he was ever thwarted or obstructed in his desire to labour in the open air.

Another of the great evangelists of a bygone era with whom Raymond had something in common was Dr. Asahel Nettleton, who was a confirmed Calvinist and greatly used of God in the period around 1812 in Connecticut, U.S.A. Charles Finney was a contemporary of Nettleton and was the forerunner of the modern day Pelagian or or Semi-Pelagian evangelists. "By his free will man is emancipated from God."* This succinct statement is the key to Pelagianism. The ability of a free will to choose good or evil and the denial of total depravity, combined with the possibility of living a sinless life — all these are implicit in the tenets of Pelagianism.

Nettleton sought to discuss with Finney, so that by consultation they might be able to co-operate and work together in promoting the welfare of the kindgom of God, but to no avail. Finney, doubtless an earnest and zealous man, has yet much to answer for in the superficiality of modern day evangelism and the universal denial of the true Pauline theology encapsulated in the doctrines of grace, commonly known as Calvinism. Nettleton faced the spread of Finney's theology with its denial of total depravity, its rejection of the doctrine of original sin with its transmission of corruption to the hearts of Adam's descendants. Indeed Finney phrases his conclusions at one point thus, "Sinners can go to hell in spite of God," adding; "Men are able to resist the utmost influence that the truth can exert upon them, and therefore have ability to defeat the wisest, most benevolent, and most powerful exertions which the Holy Spirit can make to effect their sanctification."**

---

*Baker Dictionary of Theology.
**Perfectionism, Presbyterian and Reformed Publishing Co.

So Raymond laboured in the midst of the fruits of that error which Nettleton had encountered in its resurgence in his day. Raymond was surrounded by Arminian evangelists to such extent that he could scarcely find another like-minded Calvinistic evangelist in Scotland, one who was of the reformed faith, yet made a free offer of the Gospel in Christ to men dead in trespasses and sins. The uniqueness of Raymond McKeown was that he bridged the dichotomy between the propositions that one either has life, or that one has doctrine. He demonstrated the fallacy of this thinking by showing that the two are in fact inseparable, and that the best doctrine produces the best life!

From the foregoing it can be seen that Raymond's affinity with those mentioned, apart from similarities in labours, doctrine, and holiness of life, was undergirded by a determination that permeated all their work, that of glorifying God. A high view of the sovereignty of God and keen appreciation of the inability of man, produced an overwhelming desire that in all things Christ should have the preeminence. This can be contrasted with the Arminian type of evangelism which, whether consciously or not, certainly tends to elevate man. The evangelists often come with a glowing reputation based on the numbers that have found Christ through their labours, and an almost competitive league of success is created. Spiritual power and influence is assessed numerically, so that numbers of "decisions" registered become the criterion for evaluating the authenticity of a ministry. The evils which such a system of evaluation excites are headed by the arch sin — pride.

What a refreshing and inspiring attitude Raymond manifested, where humility inhibited any claims being made which suggested personal gifts or abilities being responsible for apparent success in the work of God. At this point it might also be apposite to comment, that some contemporaries of Raymond considered that he adopted an over magnanimous attitude in granting the use of the "pulpit" in the Gospel to many who were ill-equipped in public ministry. This attitude was not traceable to any lack of discernment on his part, but to the old problem of being unable to resist the requests of less able brethren lobbying for an opportunity for themselves, or some of their less gifted friends. Raymond's rather misguided generosity, in the opinion of some of this contemporaries, sometimes deprived a disappointed congregation of his own ministry.

The charisma that attended the ministry and life of Raymond McKeown have been well varified by those who knew him personally. The faults or mistakes that he displayed were of such an insignificant nature that it is difficult to escape the charge of "hero worship" when recounting his life and this primarily the reason why such faults, though of an apparently minor nature, must be recorded. Being in a position of leadership as Raymond undoubtedly was, does incur some responsibility. The most difficult aspect of this for many might be, as it certainly was for Raymond, the possibility that rebuke or censure might have to be administered to Christian people.

Paul's charge to Timothy — "Preach the word; be instant in season, out of season; reprove rebuke, exhort with all long-suffering and doctrine." 2. Timothy 4:2 was not fully implemented by Raymond in the estimation of some of his brethren, and they considered that this lack handicapped him for advancement to real pastoral leadership. Raymond's personality was such that he consistently avoided controversy, but this was sometimes construed by some as "sitting on the fence." It was a strange quirk in Raymond that he did not shirk outspoke comment when addressing matters in the secular realm. If the rule of Scripture was that in the secular world error and offence must be rebuked and corrected, but in the spiritual world everything must be left to God, then Christian leadership would pose few problems. Greater men than Raymond have experienced difficulty in striking the right balance between moderation and rashness. Eli, the priest of God, comes to mind as demonstrating undue moderation, in his case, with his own family. Peter is probably the classic example of impetuosity, yet both were good men appointed and loved by God. Perhaps Raymond subconsciously was aware of this deficiency and the difficulty of resolving it, because he often said, "One man's tolerance is another man's compromise."

Raymond's defence of this attitude would have been that such matters should be left in the hands of God to be rectified. There is no doubt that many saints have taken matters out of God's jurisdiction and violated his sovereign prerogative by seeking to do work which is peculiar to the Holy Spirit. But though such deficiency is doubtless quite prevalent in the work of God, this does not negate the fact that God has chosen human instrumentality to further His purposes. Amos or Jeremiah would probably have been delighted to leave the correction of Israel to Jehovah alone, without being involved themselves, but God decreed otherwise.

These faults did provoke brethren at times and frustrate them when they thought that a strong word from Raymond, in a situation which required discipline for example, would have carried some weight. However, none who knew and worked with Raymond personally could ever diminish in their affection and respect for him, in spite of these flaws. If these deficiencies are set against his positive attributes, liberally listed in this narrative, they assume a quite insignificant degree of importance.

In quite another realm, Raymond exhibited at times a surprising, but understandable weakness. Occasionally he would manifest a spirit of depression to his confidants who were certainly a small minority of his overall acquaintances. He got depressed and frustrated with certain forms of authority at times and this has already been referred to by his workmate Robert Liddle. Those rather starry-eyed Christians who lived in ivory towers and were blinkered regarding much of the harsh realities of life, for example in their lack of understanding of the campaign he waged against pornography, caused frustration. The normally ebullient, resilient personality could show the strain and stress of his labours in an unguarded moment, and sometimes his close friends would console and encourage him in what was never a lengthy deviation from the usual cheerful personality. These things only highlight the humanity of the man and this very characteristic endeared him to his fellows.

If there was some lack of duty in the context of discipline and stand with the Body of Christ, this certainly did not exist in the area of his own personal family life. One or two illustrations of this demonstrate Raymond's high regard for the position of a father in a household and the strong influence that he exerted upon his family with regard to Christian principles. Sadly, many Christian parents today are showing considerable laxity in the implementing and maintenance of these principles, to the detriment of Christian family life.

One area of great tension in Christian family life can arise when the children reach the age when major decisions arise in their lives. Probably the most difficult of these is in the realm of relationships. It is not uncommon for many Christians to be attracted to and eventually marry an unconverted partner, although it might be said that there is nothing more explicitly covered in Scripture than God's attitude to an "unholy alliance." Raymond's daughter Judith became engaged to an unconverted young man, much to the concern and distress of her parents. Judith recalled this traumatic time of emotional upheaval in the following words:

"My dad had a wonderful way of presenting Christian principles even from the time we were small. He taught us tithing with our pocket money. We had to eat everything for which we had given thanks to God. Dad actually stuck pictures of Biafran famine victims (the current famine victims of the time) above the dinner table . . ."

"He also insisted upon their attendance at Sunday school — just as he insisted upon the use of soap and water, not fearing that 'force work' would necessarily turn them against either in their later years. Raymond was not much in favour of making the children endure meetings convened for adults. His principle as they grew older was to show them options open to their consideration and guide them toward what he believed was healthy Christian thinking."

There were certain things, however, which were not presented as options. Raymond had especially emphasised the folly of being "unequally yoked" and when Judith found herself in this situation she was in great distress of mind and experienced anguish in a deep consciousness that she would ultimately have to sin against the clear teaching of Scripture. Judith continued, "It was one thing to know what my father said was true and biblical, but it was another to put the matter into practice. Within four weeks of the wedding date I called it off, although in terrible agony of mind and spirit."

This was another occasion like the time her brother had his childhood accident, and when much prayer was made on behalf of the McKeown family. Violet could testify that there was no parental interference in the issue, but Judith came to her own decision on the matter and again God answered prayer.

Raymond had the unenviable task of going to Judith's fiance to explain to him, at her request, the reason why the wedding could not proceed. This was an occasion when Raymond was emotionally drained, as he spent hours with a young man who wept much, but ultimately said, "Judith is lucky to have a father like you." Perhaps there was a poignant note in this statement which was underlined by the fact that the young man was himself fatherless.

Nothing, however traumatic, was allowed to interfere with the Gospel work that Raymond felt God had entrusted to him. He had battled through many difficult times, but did not allow them to hinder his evangelistic programme. There was the occasion when his telephone had to go "ex-directory" because of the pornographic warfare, when obscene phone calls harrassed his household. The acquiring of a bad back caused him suffering and inconvenience permanently. The vicissitudes of family life, the added stress of being a shop steward with the friction that inevitably arose when engaged in confronting management with the complaints of the workforce, the continual sheer physical and mental effort required in the maintenance of the work of God, none of these things moved Raymond from his avowed intent of "preaching Christ and Him crucified." This attitude of Raymond's to pursue his calling, irrespective of circumstances, favourable or otherwise, was reflected in a passage that he often ministered to Christians from the 16th chapter of Romans. He said that it was true love which motivated the labour of Tryphena and Tryphosa, and likewise Mary and Persis who laboured much in the Lord. They abounded in the work of the Lord, motivated with a love for their fellow men. This was surely true of Raymond himself.

Barlinnie Prison, the large grim and forbidding penal institution that dominates the skyline in the Riddrie district of Glasgow, has had a Gospel witness for many years. Gordon Haxton, at present in charge of the evangelistic work there, can span over 35 years service and was responsible for inviting Raymond to bring groups to sing and preach the Word of God over several years. "I first met Raymond," Gordon said, "in the back of an old Open Air Mission van about 1947. We were going down to Saltcoats on the Ayrshire coast, to the opening rally of the summer mission there. At that time the Open Air Mission evangelist was Christy Gunn. (Raymond then being about 22 years of age). Now this was the first time I had come across the man and I immediately became aware that he was full of humour and good fun and because of this, the journey was quite memorable."

The open air meeting at Glasgow Cross had just finished and Raymond spoke to some of the team and suggested that they might like to join him the following Sunday for the Bible Class at Barlinnie prison. A small musical group was always popular with the prisoners, especially in the days before they had access to television, snooker and various recreational activities, which now make it harder to get them out to a Gospel service. "Meet me about 2.25 on Sunday afternoon," Raymond said, "and we should be in good time for the service."

The following Sunday, about half a dozen members of the team congregated outside the huge green metal gates at the entrance to the prison. Raymond remarked to the group, "These fellas inside think we're soft, that we're mugs who are taken in by religion. But, just ask yourself, 'Who will be the mugs that will be coming back out through these gates in an hour's time'?" There was a ripple of laughter which contrasted with the shiver of apprehension that ran through some of the Christians who had never been inside a prison before. Here they were entering the infamous Barlinnie, home for all kinds of criminals, ranging from murderers to bank robbers, rapists to confidence men and including the whole spectrum of lawbreakers. The party was ushered into the gatehouse where they signed the register, were counted and then waited for a phone call from the gymnasium which would inform the prison officer who would accompany them, that the prisoners were ready and seated for the service. Being a cold day, the visiting party gathered around a cosy, warm coal fire in the gatehouse, and when the phone call came, they left the warmth of the gatehouse to proceed to the courtyard to the gymnasium building. The prisoners, about eighty in number, dressed in drab khaki uniform and guarded by several prison officers, looked round expectantly when the party entered.

Gordon Haxton and the organist were well known to the prisoners, but Raymond and the other visitors were viewed with a mixture of curiosity and resignation. They were prepared to suffer some religion, just to relieve the monotony of cell life, where many were cramped with two other prisoners for most of their jail sentence. Strapping on the accordion, Raymond was soon into his winning routine of quipping and joking as he broke the ice and soon had them won over. He kept the preaching simple, but rivetted their attention nevertheless. On one occasion he said, "You know, fellas, you can run away from home, from a heartbroken mother, you can even run away from the law for a while, but you cannot run away from God! Look at old Jonah there! Running away from God, and what do we find? Running down to Joppa to go to Tarshish. Then what do we find? He's going down into the depths of a ship! The next thing is that he's thrown overboard down into the tempestuous sea and a great fish swallows him, and down, down he goes into its belly! Aye, the only place a man can go when he runs from God, is down, down, down!''

Simple, but effective, because there was utmost sincerity in the deliverance of an almost childlike Sunday school message, but it came from a ''master craftsman'' of a preacher, who, like his Master, was prepared to make himself of no reputation, if by any means he might point some to salvation.

''Dunky'' Donaldson had been an inmate in Barlinnie prison and, in fact, had over a hundred convictions for various offences. Although Raymond had not visited Barlinnie while Dunky was incarcerated there, the two met at the Barrowland market, very soon after Dunky was convicted of his need of Christ. Here he describes his first meeting with Raymond in his own words: ''When I was just a few weeks saved, I had an old brown suit which I had bought in a pawnshop.'' In his own inimitable way, Dunky, with a broad Glasgow accent, described his sartorial elegance in the vernacular as ''An auld broon suit, bought oot o' the poanshoap wi' troosers that wir too big!'' He continued, ''I heard Raymond preach at Glasgow Cross and the Barrows for the first time and although I knew nothing of the Scriptures then, just listening to the 'wee man' was brilliant!'' Dunky went on, ''The crowd that were with him were magic too, the way they played and sang the Gospel. I never heard anything like it in my whole life.'' Quoting a famous Scottish ballad, he said, '''O Flower of Scotland, when shall we see your likes again.' I wouldn't have missed knowing Raymond for anything, and I've thanked God for the fellows who took me and introduced me to him.'' Dunky could say that he never once went to the open airs after his introduction to Raymond, but what the 'wee man', as he called him, asked him to give his testimony. ''I couldn't preach for two pence, but Raymond would call me up to the microphone and I would be shouting 'Hallelujah! Love lifted me.' It used to be the police that 'lifted' me, but now the Lord has lifted me, glory to His name!''

It seemed most appropriate that Dunky should accompany Raymond back to Barlinnie Prison on occasion and this he did several times. Many of the prisoners knew that in his day, this was the wildest man in Airdrie, and that it took six policemen to arrest him and drag him to the town jail on a Friday night after a drinking spree! The change in Dunky was so radical and dramatic that his former associates could hardly believe it was the same man!

When the "rough diamonds" of life are converted it is sometimes apparent that grace has still much work to do in their sanctification. Dunky reminisced about a particular incident which illustrates this. "I remember one Sunday afternoon at the Barrows we were continually tormented and insulted by a radical socialist who was just there to make trouble. Raymond carried on in his own serene way, ignoring the jibes and insults or occasionally making an apt reply. One new Christian who had also come from a real bad background was getting very frustrated by the interruptions and insults, and remedied this by planting a right hook on the jaw of the offender which knocked him totally unconscious. When the victim came to his senses, he complained bitterly to Raymond about being assaulted by a Christian. Raymond, after sympathising with the man, said, 'Yes, I perfectly understand, son, that it was a Christian who hit you today. However, you can be thankful that he was a Christian — otherwise he would probably have hit you six months ago'!" Dunky went on from what may have been a tale with apocryphal tendencies to confirm the sheer philanthropic nature of the man, by telling how in visitations to preach in City Missions, Raymond, more often than not, slipped some financial gift to the Superintendents who were in straitened circumstances, rather than receive any gratuity for his preaching.

Reflecting on the visits to Barlinnie Prison, Dunky recalled, "Once there was a woman there when I first got saved who did some singing. Raymond said to me, 'She's a faithful soul who has come here for 23 years.' 'Ach', I said, 'by the way she's singing that hymn, she should have been locked in here for 23 years!' Aye, it was good to have a laugh and a joke together, but you know, when a man like Raymond McKeown could get through with the Gospel to a man like me, 'drunken Duncan,' now that's something special.

I wouldn't be a Christian today if it hadn't been for Raymond and the ministry at the Barrows. When I got saved I couldn't believe that going to the meeting on a Sunday and once in the middle of the week was all there was to do for a Christian. So I asked, 'Well, whit dae wi dae noo! Is this aw thir is fur us tae dae in a week?''

99

Nobody could tell me anything else that I could actively have been doing for the Lord the other days of the week.'' Dunky made it patently obvious that mere attendance at meetings was not sufficient to satisfy the desire he felt to tell the world what the Saviour had done for him. The Glasgow Cross and Barrows open air meetings provided the vehicle for him, and many like him, to express their faith to the world at large, to reach sinners just where they were in their everyday circumstances. There is no doubt about it, Raymond's ministry in this respect was indispensable for new converts like Dunky and others from completely different backgrounds, who had a need to express their faith to those who seldom darkened the door of a church. ''That wee man was a real Christian, a gem. I don't think we'll see his like again!'' A fitting tribute from one of God's more unique ''trophies of grace!''

Chapter 10

Ministry Amongst the Gaels

Gardner Street in Partick flows down to Dumbarton Road like some dark stream through a cavern of grey sandstone tenement buildings. Commencing high at the north end, it rapidly descends in an exceedingly steep gradient, to level out a little before joining the main road. Situated at the bottom end of the street, with a rather forbidding exterior, is Gardner Street Church of Scotland, a quite unique place of worship in Glasgow. It is here that Gaelic people have congregated to worship since the Gaelic Mission was established to cater for Highland Scots around 1875.

The Pass of the Cattle ascends from sea level to 2,054 feet in Wester Ross, making it one of the highest roads in Britain. The wild, zig zagging road seems to climb endlessly through breathtaking scenic views before reaching the summit of Bealach na Ba, the Gaelic name for the pass. The superlative view that unfolds as the eye ranges over the magical vista of the Hebridean seascape, explains the nostalgic longing that such conjures up in the heart of expatriate Scots worldwide. On a good day, the Western island of Skye with the impressive Cuillin mountains dominates the view. From the summit, if the eye follows the winding road down to Applecross village and beyond over the Inner Sound, the isles of Raasay, Rona, and Scalpay can be seen. The mountain road quickly descends to Applecross and virtually flows into the sea with Applecross perching on the edge of the penninsula from which it gets its name. St. Maelrubha, one of the Irish missionaries reputed to have brought Christianity to Scotland, founded a monastery at Applecross in AD 673, and his grave is marked with a stone cross.

Kenneth Gillies was born in Applecross in 1886 and like so many Gaels from the northwest of Scotland, he came south to Glasgow as a teenager at the beginning of this century. The number of Highland youths who made a career in the Glasgow Police Force virtually made the Force their own. While he was a constable in the police, Kenneth attended Gardner Street church and was converted through the preaching of his own minister from Applecross, the Rev. Angus MacIver, who happened to be visiting preacher on that occasion. Sensing a call to the ministry himself, Kenneth Gillies was eventually inducted to that very charge of Gardner Street church in 1924, the year before Raymond McKeown was born in Belfast.

The Gaels have a tendency to keep to themselves and are not generally noted for being particularly outgoing in matters of religion. Kenneth Gillies had a true catholic spirit and his ministry was not confined to the denomination which he represented, but true evangelical zeal caused him to fellowship with Christians of many persuasions. Gardner Street church, being situated in the heart of Partick, it seems inevitable that two great servants of God like Kenneth Gillies and Raymond McKeown would meet and fellowship together. Kenneth Gillies, because of his wide interest in evangelical work, was a not infrequent visitor to the Tent Hall in Glasgow. Raymond was working in the Tent Hall at that time and Kenneth Gillies was impressed by his ministry and character and invited him to fill the pulpit on occasions when he would be visiting other congregations. Eventually, having seen the quality of Raymond's ministry, Kenneth Gillies asked him to consider a post as "assistant to the minister" in the Gardner Street church.

The work load at Gardner Street was heavy and consisted of four services on a Sunday, bible study on a Wednesday and a prayer meeting on Saturday. Being primarily the church for Gaelic speaking Highland Scots who had migrated to Glasgow for jobs, it had a bi-lingual ministry of English and Gaelic. It was for the English ministry on Sundays that Raymond was enlisted. He would preach alternately on morning and evening each Sunday. It does not require much imagination to realise that there was a tremendous contrast between the open air ministry with its swashbuckling extempore and eclectic approach, and the rather sombre and restrained atmosphere of the Highland form of worship practised at Gardner Street. From Stornoway, Skye and the Western Isles generally they congregated at Gardner Street. The mainland Scotland was represented by the north west coast and the descendants of the Gaels now domiciled in and around Glasgow. Men there were present who had known the breath of genuine revival in the Isle of Lewis when the Spirit of God had moved in mighty power and conviction in answer to prevailing prayer.

Raymond would sometimes reflect on the spiritual experience of many in the congregation before he entered the pulpit. There were not too many churches in the land who had members with first-hand knowledge and experience of genuine revival. On one occasion in the early sixties, a special meeting was convened in the old Tolbooth Mission at Glasgow Cross which had been addressed by Duncan Campbell, a minister whom God had used significantly in the revival of 1949. Raymond often thought how the meeting had been charged with the power of the Holy Spirit as Duncan Campbell recounted some of the events of the time. Aye, they were a canny lot, these Gaels, Raymond reflected, but it had to be admitted that they seemed to enjoy seasons of refreshing in revivings that the rest of the U.K. had not experienced.

The Open Air Team workers listened fascinated that Saturday in the Tolbooth Mission as Duncan Campbell first told of his own conversion and how the intercession of praying parents played a major role in his going into an old barn beside the croft situated in the Campbell clan territory of Argyll to cry to God for mercy. He was saved kneeling amidst the straw and rose to share the news with his parents and turn his back on the pleasures of the world for evermore. His account of the awakening in the Isle of Lewis gripped the hearers. Some of them had read his book, "God's Answer," which contained an extract from the Stornoway Gazette in 1949 which showed the spiritual condition of the island at that time.

> "The decline referred to in this declaration began to show itself in a growing disregard for the things of God; indeed the blighting influence of the spirit of the age, with its deadening effect, had wrought so effectively that in certain parishes very few young people attended public worship: the dance, the picture show and the drinking house were institutions which could now thrive in Lewis, on the generous support given by their willing devotees."

"The movement that began in the Parish Church of Barvas, almost immediately spread to the neighbouring Parish of Ness, and it soon became evident that it was not to be confined to these two parishes. From north, south, east and west the people came in buses, vans, cars and lorries, to witness the mighty movings of God and then to return to their respective parishes to bear testimony to the fact that they had met with the Saviour. A gamekeeper, whose home was twenty four miles from Barvas, was so wrought upon and burdened for the souls of others, that his van was seldom off the road and for two years, night after night, brought its load of men and women who were seeking for Jesus. He was rewarded by seeing many come to the Saviour, including members of his own family. It is therefore not surprising that in the Parish of Lochs, where the gentleman referred to had his home, a gracious movement should break out."*

Such were the personal experiences of some of the members in the Gardner Street congregation. Whenever Raymond mounted the pulpit stairs, accompanied by Mr. Gillies, his mind turned often to the subject of revival. This was inevitable because he looked out upon many who had experienced a mighty sweep of the Spirit in the far off churches in Lewis. The knowledge that Duncan Campbell, so used of God in the revival, had been in the same pulpit, continually fuelled Raymond's own desire to see such a move of God in mainland Scotland.

Kenneth Gillies was already in his "eighties" as he sat beside Raymond, in the pulpit of the church where he had ministered for fifty years or so. He sat with quiet appreciation of the versatility that Raymond showed in repeatedly presenting a children's message that never failed to enthrall. But now Raymond had announced his text for the morning message and Kenneth Gillies settled back to enjoy a careful exposition of the Word of God. "This morning, our text is Malachi 3:6 'For I am the Lord, I change not; therefore ye sons of Jacob are not consumed.' Three very, very important things are said about the basic reality of the Christian faith in this text of Scripture: it speaks of God, the Being of God — I am the Lord. In the second place it speaks of the immutability of God, the unchangeableness of God — 'I am the Lord I change not'; and in the third place it speaks of the Grace of God — 'I am the Lord I change not, therefore ye sons of Jacob are not consumed.' Three very important things that Christian people should know in these days!

First of all — the Being of God. 'I am the Lord.' Secondly, the immutability of God, the unchangeableness of God, 'I change not.' And thirdly, the grace of God; 'therefore ye sons of Jacob are not consumed.' In very measured and deliberate style, Raymond thus

---

*God's Answer. Faith Mission Publications.

addressed the Gardner Street congregation. Not many of them had actually witnessed Raymond in action at Glasgow Cross in the open air. They would have been astonished at the complete contrast of his indoor pulpit style. Likewise, the thronging crowds who often listened at Barrowland Market would never have recognised the ministerial tone or quiet seriousness of "the assistant to the minister" of Gardner Street church. The taciturn, apparently unemotional Gaels listened with rapt attention and were as much captivated by this Raymond as were the Clydeside working-class with Raymond the open air preacher.

He continued his exposition by saying: "What then does the text say about the Being of God? The text speaks very plainly of God as a personality. 'I am the Lord.' And here we have the biblical answer to atheism, which denies the existence of God. 'I am the Lord,' we have the biblical answer to pantheism which says that God is not personality, but God is an influence inherent in all things. The Bible here says, 'I am the Lord,' not a pervasive influence, but 'I am the Lord.' We have the answer here to agnosticism, which says that God, if He exists, cannot be known, for the Bible here is saying that God is making Himself known in self-revelation. This is not man seeking after God, man trying to find God, this is God coming to man in a self-revelation. And so we have the answer here to the three great objections to the Christian God. To the objection of atheism which says that God does not exist, it makes a positive statement. Here is the answer to pantheism which speaks of God in this manner 'I am the Lord,' and, the answer to agnosticism is in this text, as it speaks of God revealing Himself in a very definite way."

Those who appreciated the ministry of Raymond McKeown and Kenneth Gillies could never have anticipated at the beginning of 1975 that before another year concluded the ministries of both these outstanding servants of God would be a matter of history. The increasingly ecumenical drift of the Church of Scotland, especially with its overtures to Rome, became a source of embarrassment to Raymond, and, in his opinion, weakened and compromised his testimony. The decision to resign from Gardner Street was not taken hastily or without heart searching, but painful though it was, he ceased his association with them on 1st June, 1975.

"The Session would like to place on record its deep gratitude for the much valued contribution you have made to the congregation's life and witness during the years in which it has been privileged to enjoy your fellowship — for a richly edifying pulpit ministry, for a captivating and winsome presentation of the Gospel to the Sunday School children, for your faithful support of the prayer meeting, and for all the stimulus and encouragement you have given to young believers."

This is an extract from a letter written by Kenneth MacDonald, Session Clerk of Gardner Street church, with Christian love, on behalf of the Kirk Session and Congregation.

In August, 1976 Raymond was one of many who penned tributes to Kenneth Gillies, who passed to his rest in his 90th year, having been the longest-serving minister in the Church of Scotland. A remarkable 52 years of consecutive ministry, which only terminated about a year before his death, was unique in his denomination and probably any other church in the land. Raymond wrote a tribute to the Stornoway Gazette which catered specially for the Gaelic community far beyond the confines of the Isle of Lewis itself. A portion of his euology to his old friend is reproduced here:

"After 52 years of ministry in a congregation where four services are held every Sunday, with a mid-week service every Wednesday and a prayer meeting every Saturday, a work load to daunt men half his age, Mr. Gillies maintained the loyalty and affection of a loving congregation.

He was a friend of evangelical causes. He was for many years a director of the Glasgow Evangelical Association. He supported many missionary societies and was a regular visitor to the Keswick Convention and to the Northern Convention in Strathpeffer. He was also a member of the Presbytery of Glasgow. He was a faithful churchman, a good Presbyter, a zealous minister, a sympathetic and diligent pastor, and, above all, a man greatly beloved. He adorned his office, he died as he lived in Christ."

So ended an era in Gardner Street which was notable for having two outstanding, though diverse ministries working in tandem for many years. Certainly there was a tremendous contrast between the two men in every way. Physically, Kenneth Gillies was tall and erect; Raymond small and burly. In preaching delivery, the former was slow and precise, without the animation or rhetoric that Raymond possessed. Both had their roots deep in Celtic heritage and their providential coming together and successful blending of two distinctive ministries is not surprising if one traces the Scottish and Irish Presbyterian tradition to its sources.

The unfathomable mysteries of Providence which finally united Kenneth Gillies and Raymond McKeown in the Gospel ministry at Gardner Street, could be traced back through the mists of time to the Ards peninsula, which geographically is the closest part of the Irish mainland to Scotland. Most of the settlers were doughty Presbyterians, and, by the middle of the 17th century, there was quite an influx of them spreading out into County Down and County Antrim. the very remoteness of Ireland as an island contributed much to the fact of it being largely unaffected by the Reformation. However, due to the success of the Protestant Reformation in Britain, the effects gradually reached Ireland. Such was the historical background from which the McKeowns sprang. It would not stretch credulity over-much to imagine that men from the Presbyterian stock from which the Gillies family was derived, were amongst those who peopled Ireland back in these early days and were fellow citizens of Ulster with the McKeowns. The ramifications of Providence are beyond imagination, but its intricate weaving of events through time and history, which ultimately produces such an association of God's elect in a modern scenario, is indeed compelling drama.

That Providence was determined to return Raymond to the land of his nativity, was confirmed by the persistence of the Templemore assembly in Belfast to call him as their pastor. Their first approach in 1965 had been unsuccessful but changing circumstances added more weight and persuasiveness to their renewed appeal in 1981. Raymond had been retired due to ill health, in the form of a bad back, since 1979. The diminishing interest in open air work by the general public who now had the finest entertainment and sports presented to them through the medium of television, was disheartening to him. Another matter which caused him some despondency was the lack of any sign of true revival, for which he nurtured a burning desire to the end of his life. Around this time Raymond expressed his sense of frustration and measure of discontent to a friend during a lengthy discussion on the nature of biblical faith and the recognition of a genuine call of God. In spite of being somewhat unsettled at this time, his zeal never diminished for the work of God. In 1981 Raymond was photographed holding a placard aloft which proclaimed his opposition to a local Sex Shop and indeed a campaign largely orchestrated by him was reported in a national newspaper headline which read, "No Sex Please! Glasgow's first sex shop was stripped within two hours of opening yesterday. In a mid-morning raid six policemen denuded the shelves." A prolific amount of letters flowed from his pen against this trade and his open air output was still considerable. But the "magic" had gone! All the ability, all the oratory was still there but the populace now had little ear for the Gospel, even from a "master craftsman."

In 1981, after several attempts, the Templemore Assembly oversight requested a meeting with Raymond. A date was finally set for March, 1982, and the meeting duly took place and the visiting brethren carried a unanimous recommendation back to Belfast that Templemore Hall should invite Raymond to the pastoral office of the Assembly. At this particular time, he had been unemployed for three years due to back trouble, and, although he was greatly frustrated by the uncertainty of the future, yet he was also grateful to God for the additional time at his disposal for study and prayer. Having previously turned down an invitation to Templemore Hall, Raymond and Violet gave serious consideration to the call, resisting any temptation to make a hasty decision. It was difficult to be totally objective in the matter because the existing circumstances, with their great degree of uncertainty, could exert undue pressure to accept merely as a means to relieve the situation. Just prior to the invitation coming, Raymond had casually remarked to Violet one evening, "Do you realise, Violet, that all our anchor lines are being loosened? Your father has now been taken care of in the nursing home, Paul and Judith are off our hands now with a home of their own, I have no secular job to tie me down and even you have no vocational or spiritual calling to make it necessary for you to remain in Glasgow. I just feel somehow that God is loosing our anchor lines for some specific purpose."

So when the invitation came it was against this background that they prayed regarding God's will in the matter. Eventually, although Violet had some reluctance initially because of the family ties, grandchildren and the like, nevertheless they finally agreed that it seemed to be the Lord's leading for them to go to Belfast and take up this new and challenging ministry. Raymond had been standing in for some months as interim pastor in Clydebank Baptist church and soon after accepting the Templemore Hall call, the Baptist church invited him to the pastorate on a permanent basis, but the die was cast. Raymond and Violet began preparations for what was to prove the last chapter in Raymond's earthly ministry.

Chapter 11

Back To Belfast

Belfast 1982 found Raymond returning to the land of his nativity. The "Troubles" that drove his parents into exile some fifty odd years ago, had continued to ferment in the Province ever since. It does seem that the Irish, as one of their own politicians so aptly put it, "are prisoners of history." Raymond had made repeated visits to Northern Ireland over the years, so he was in touch with the pulse of things and he quickly settled into the pattern there after his induction to Templemore Hall.

Violet later spoke of these first days in Belfast with a nostalgic note: "You know how Raymond was. He had had hardly settled into our new home or the work at Templemore Hall until he was foraging the city for the best open air meeting sites. The confines of Templemore could not contain his free spirit and very soon he was in contact with a small missionary group called Youth Evangelical Missionary Fellowship, which existed primarily to motivate young people for foreign missionary work. Before long he was engaged every Tuesday morning lecturing to his group on an informal basis. This gave him the opportunity of meeting young people of various nationalities, which was a great joy to him." Violet warmed to the recounting of this particular aspect of his initial ministry in Belfast by continuing, "Apparently, one morning, Raymond was so engrossed in his address to the students that he was leaning back precariously on his chair and, on making a specifically vehement point, toppled over backwards, to the amused consternation of the assembled audience. It was a lecture which they did not forget quickly!" In a more serious vein, Violet subsequently received a grateful letter from two Nigerian students after his death, saying how much he had encouraged and instructed them at these lectures. This was typical of the response generated there.

In the middle of a shopping precinct in Belfast city centre there is a place called the Corn Market. This was the location much frequented by all classes of society. Punk rockers could be found mingling with ordinary housewives, business men with the unemployed, and it became Raymond's first venue for Saturday afternoon open air meetings. The successful methodology, so blessed of God during the many years of open air work in Clydeside, was utilised again in the streets of Belfast. The amplifier and microphone were connected, the accordion strapped on and the familiar strains of the old Gospel hymns rang out in that clear tenor voice that the Glasgow crowds knew and appreciated down through many years. The fact that there has been unprecedented response to the Gospel in Northern Ireland historically, also meant there were many backsliders mingling with the crowd at the Corn Market. Raymond regularly had some feedback regarding how many backsliders who had given up attending church would be standing listening to the open air meeting. On Monday evenings in the summertime, Raymond also conducted an open air meeting in the Templemore Hall locality and at all of these was ably assisted by John Jordan, who had a great bass singing voice, and an increasing number of the church members.

When Raymond had been interviewed with regard to filling the vacancy in the church, he made a statement during the discussion, which one brother said would remain with him all his life. "Gentlemen, this task is too much for me. I'm not a big enough man for this. I'll play second fiddle to somebody, or take on the open air work. The pastorate is too much." This made a tremendous impact on the brethren at the meeting, because they knew that most applicants would probably have jumped at the chance to be appointed. As one of them remarked later, "Here is one of the few men we have ever met who is not conscious of his true worth.'

The challenge presented by the open air ministry was soon to become a challenge to the reality of practical Chrisianity to many of the Templemore Hall membership. This challenge manifested in a way that few could have envisaged before Raymond's coming into the midst. Once the Saturday and Monday open air services were established, Raymond turned his attention to the immediate vicinity of the church. He felt a burden to carry the Gospel to all sectors of the community, including the Roman Catholic populace and, it was because of this, that he dropped a bombshell in the midst of the assembly.

Sharing his concern with responsible brethren one evening, he

111

suggested that they should consider evangelising the area adjacent to the hall. There was a pregnant silence as the implication of this remark sunk in. The reason for this was that the area referred to by Raymond was the Short Strand, an inviolate Republican stronghold. To those unaquainted with the political and religious complexities of Ulster politics, it might seem amazing that Ravenhill Road, which is virtually a continuation of the Short Strand, should be a Unionist and Protestant stronghold, with the line of demarcation virtually unseen by the casual observer. Suffice it to say, however, that Raymond's shattering suggestion stopped the discussion in its track! One brother timorously suggested, "Raymond, if we go down there we could easily be shot and killed." Quietly and without the slightest suggestion of bravado or rebuke, Raymond replied softly, "Brother, I thought that the Gospel we believed in was worth dying for!" There was no answer to that and it was agreed that an open air meeting should be conducted in the Short Strand for the first time in living memory by the folks in Templemore Hall.

Raymond had known religious bigotry in Glasgow where it took on a particularly unique form. The Protestant and Roman Catholic dichotomy was never more vociferously articulated by the mob, than when the two leading soccer teams met in regular combat. Protestantism was represented by Glasgow Rangers club and Roman Catholicism by Glasgow Celtic club. Glasgow Rangers' tradition was that they had never signed a Catholic during the club's history and, even at the time of writing, no "Fenian" has pulled on a blue jersey. The Celtic club have not been so discriminatory, and many Protestants have been adorned with the green and white jersey, although this probably owed as much to pragmatism as a more enlightened attitude. This is demonstrated by the fact that Protestantism has regularly been provoked by the flying of the Eire flag from the Parkhead flagstaff. All the worst features of sectarian bigotry and violence have occurred in clashes between the teams at both Ibrox stadium, home of Rangers, and Parkhead stadium, Celtic's ground. Any deposit of true religion in either faction would be hard to find.

This kind of attitude is found in much of the intolerance and bigotry that exists amongst some in Northern Ireland. Unfortunately, the general public and media find it impossible to recognise that, although dead Protestantism and dead Catholicism are both abhorrent in God's estimation, yet there is an evangelical

Protestantism which is biblical, commendable and totally divorced from the religious or political parody which bears its name.

So as the Shankill and Sandy Row maintain the Protestant tradition, likewise the Lower Falls and Ardoyne are Republican citadels. In these working-class sections the antagonists keep strictly to their own turf, yet there are many other areas in Belfast of a middle-class tendency, where no such divide exists.

The import of Raymond's suggestion concerning Short Strand can be more fully appreciated in the light of these factors. Some apprehension undoubtedly existed before the first venture into the Short Strand, but Raymond was quietly confident that it was God's direction and therefore He would undertake. The little band of workers followed Raymond for the first meeting into the Short Strand, an epoch they were not to forget easily. As often happens, the actual event was something of an anti-climax insofar as anything dramatic in the way of opposition occurring. Raymond summoned up his wealth of experience in all kinds of open air meetings and adopted a very low key approach. A few well known Gospel hymns, a heavy emphasis on music and singing, and a brief message had the curious peering out from behind curtained windows, or the downright inquisitive boldly staring from their front doors. One or two spoke briefly to them and gave the impression that they would be welcome to come again. Gradually they won the people's confidence and the children especially crowded round, attracted by the music and singing. The master craftsman had lost none of his charisma and if he happened to miss a week because of other business, some of the old ladies would come out and say "Where have you been? We've missed you."

Around Christmas 1982, the group decided to concentrate on singing some carols, and this was wonderfully received by their regular hearers. Indeed one old lady in her eighties came across to the party and slipped a five pound note into Raymond's hand as he played the accordion, saying, "Bless you son, that's the best I've heard for a long time." He had to go over to her house and return the gift and this gave him an opportunity bring a brief testimony of God's grace to the occupants. Minor incidents like this nevertheless confirmed his conviction that the Gospel, simply stated, transcended all divides — political, racial or religious.

Val English, a lecturer at Belfast Bible College, first met Raymond at the Bangor Missionary Conference. He was greatly impressed by the consummate ease with which Raymond conducted the meetings at the Sunken Gardens on the sea front of the popular seaside resort. The background to his ministry necessitates the insertion of the testimony of Mr. Herbert Mateer, who is well known in Northern Ireland for his founding of the famous Bangor Worldwide Missionary Convention of which he was secretary for many years. Herbert Mateer recalled his introduction to Raymond in Belfast in this way:

"I happened to be passing the City Hall in Belfast one Saturday night when I was attracted to a lively open air meeting in front of the hall. I was immediately drawn to the meeting because I had myself previously started open air meetings near this location. Now, I did not know who the speaker was, neither could I recall ever having seen him before. I was so impressed by his ministry that I made enquiries as to who he was and where he came from." Herbert went on, "It was a very short time after that I approached Raymond about the possibility of holding open air meetings in conjunction with the Missionary Conference. This was a new departure and it seemed a good idea to hold evangelistic services while missionaries and supporters from all over the world were gathered together. Now we were so pleased with Raymond and his ministry that we invited him back year after year so that he completed almost twenty years consecutive preaching there, commencing around 1964."

A typical day at the Conference commenced with a prayer meeting from ten till eleven each week day morning. After a cup of coffee and some fellowship, many of the participants would go down to the foot of Main Street, on the sea front, at eleven thirty, for the Gospel open air meetings, which concluded at twelve thirty. On a Sunday there was a special site for the Sunday afternoon open air when hundreds could be gathered at the Pickie Pool overlooking the town. The presence of such a crowd, the beautiful surroundings, the joy of being in the company of many godly missionaries and friends, so motivated Raymond that the anointing of the Spirit seemed even more to rest upon him and the ministry.

Herbert continued his recollections, saying: "In the forty odd years that I was secretary of the Conference, we had up to forty missionary societies represented on occasions, but none had the gift in the open air like Raymond. I recall on the last occasion that he was with us that on two consecutive mornings at the Sunken Gardens, he gave two addresses which I shall never forget — from Isa. 42:3. The first

114

message was, 'A bruised reed shall he not break.' The second was, 'The smoking flax shall he not quench.' I have said to many people that I never heard a better exposition at Keswick, Port Stewart or at the Bangor Conventions than I did on these two mornings on the sea front at the Sunken Gardens. Jock Troup, Raymond's spiritual father, came for twelve years to the Bangor Convention, and in my opinion was the greatest open air preacher I have ever heard until Raymond came on the scene.''

Val English was not alone in being captivated by the unique magic of Raymond's open air ministry. They soon came together because he was also interested in such work and instantly recognised a master craftsman when he heard one. Val especially remembered Raymond's peculiar skill in conducting the open air meeting at Bangor, so that when Raymond suggested they might do some open air work together in Belfast, he readily agreed. It was not long before Val recognised the depth of ability Raymond had in other areas of ministry and he soon invited him to come along to Belfast Bible College during his first year at Templemore Hall. The idea was for Raymond to do a series of lectures on evangelism with some emphasis on open air work. Val put it this way: ''I then discovered that he was not just a gifted open air preacher, but had a tremendous way with the students. He challenged and presented them with so many facets of truth and dealt admirably with matters theological and philosophical. He would set forth arguments and refutations which would help the students to cope with objections brought against them in their presentation of the Gospel, especially in the open air, or personal witness. As a result of this, the students loved him and though he came along to the College for only two or three weeks in the year, his work was invaluable.''

Val English cited various examples where Raymond had personally taken some individual students under his wing and encouraged and developed their ministries. In the somewhat controversial area of women's ministry, Raymond had encouraged some of the girl students to develop their gifts within the contest of a local church situation but without usurping traditional or orthodox evangelical standards, apart from those of a more extreme position. Val English expressed his opinion of Raymond's contribution in this realm thus, ''I think if many of the students with whom Raymond had contact were given the opportunity to speak of their association with him they would testify that they had come to pastoral understanding and experience, insights into people, a grasp of temperaments and greater ability in coping with various trouble situations. These understandings came as a result of their exposure to Raymond's advice and help. Raymond McKeown had that rare pastoral gift, not only evidenced in his preaching, but in his relationships with people and not just involvement with them but getting them motivated in the work of God. I think that he was a true subscriber to the principle of the priesthood of all believers.''

Raymond had a close and warm relationship with one of the great "characters" of the Irish evangelical scene called Jimmy Carson. Collecting "characters" seemed to be one of Raymond's perennial qualities and he continued this habit in Ireland, as he had done in Scotland. Jimmy Carson would have found tremendous rapport with Tommy Campbell, one of Raymond's Glasgow "worthies." They were both men of an indomitable praying spirit. Jimmy was crude, rough and primitive in his approach to prayer but there was reverence, faith and total sincerity there. He believed in taking the kingdom of heaven by violence by single minded supplication. Writing to Raymond one day from Carrickfergus, he penned these words:,

> My Dear Brother,
> Oh for a revival of Holy Ghost conviction of sin and a Holy Ghost revelation of what it means to be born again! My conviction, brother, as I wait upon God and His Word, is that thousands who believe they are saved and born again will end up in Hell, with God's voice ringing in their ears — 'Depart from me I never knew you.' Raymond, I am so ashamed of the hours I have spent in bed feeling tired and used the time for laziness. Oh, brother, never forget about yourself in these areas. Check up with God, Amen!''

Jimmy would never have won a prize for literary excellence or cultural refinement, but Raymond esteemed him a choice servant and his influence on Raymond can be seen in the following pastoral excerpts.

To say that Raymond McKeown was a "human dynamo" seems an understatement when considering the output of pastoral visitation, preaching engagements, open air work, crusading against obscenity and pornography and the ordinary, though time-consuming activity of fellowshipping with Christians of various denominations. Many of the Templemore Hall congregation had their own personal stories of Raymond's unceasing devotion to pastoral care far beyond the bounds of normal duty. A few short extracts illustrate the matter: One sister could say,

"My daughter's father-in-law was an alcoholic and when he went on a binge he always sent for me. I introduced him to Raymond McKeown who really took him upon his heart. He came to Templemore Hall occasionally, although he was not really interested in the Gospel — but he was interested in Raymond McKeown as a man. On the last occasion he went off on an alcoholic spree, his wife and family left him and he sent for me to come and help him. After I had spoken to him about the things of God he asked if Raymond McKeown would come to him, which he did after the evening prayer meeting. He stayed until midnight, then left to return to the Hall for prayer until the early hours of the morning after which he came back and stayed the remainder of the night helping this man. My own father was in a mental hospital and Raymond visited him every week for over two years. On the day he died I arrived at the hospital to find Raymond already there, holding his hand."

Another lady said: "My husband had been an alcoholic before his conversion and sadly sometimes he fell back to the drink. Raymond was wonderful in coming round to the house and saying, 'Now it's one thing to fall down, but another to get up again, so just don't lie there, but get up and go on.' He gave great encouragement such as we never found anywhere else. It just seemed that we could not tell of this dilemma to anyone else, because there is an attitude with many that once you're saved you should never have recurrence of such a problem. Since Mr. McKeown went to be with the Lord we have got off the fence and started to serve God in the way that he had been exhorting us to do. My sixteen-year-old son was restored to the Lord during Raymond's ministry, having been into glue sniffing and many of the escapades that youngsters get involved with today. Once when my daughter had a very bad car accident, she was actuallay pronounced dead at first, but was resuscitated by a policeman at the scene of the accident. When I got to the hospital and was standing anxiously at the bedside, I turned around and there was Mr. McKeown standing at my side. He was a father, a counsellor and shining example to us all."

Another member of Templemore congregation had this to say about Raymond:

"Mr. McKeown hadn't been long at the Hall and my wife had not met him because she had been confined to bed with back trouble.

Raymond came to me and said, 'I hear that your wife isn't keeping too well, so I'll try and come round on Monday afternoon.' Sure enough, on Monday afternoon, the doorbell went and there was Raymond. My wife was lying on the settee when he came into the room and gave a cheery 'hello!' I pointed to a chair, but he said, 'I'm fine' and he sat on the floor beside the couch, took her hand and said, 'Now come on, sister, tell me all about yourself.' After having a talk with her he said, 'You're awful depressed, love. I think you need a wee bit cheering up, Do you mind if I go down to my car and bring up my accordion?' So, in a moment he was back with the accordion and, saying, 'Right now, love, what's your favourite chorus?' My wife said, 'He Lives,' and off he went, singing and playing for about half an hour or so. When he left, I realised that it was better than having half a dozen doctors attending her, because it just changed her attitude completely in that short space of time! My wife said, 'Oh the Lord really sent that man. What a blessing he was'."

These are just random, uncomplicated testimonies from ordinary folks who ultimately comprise the greater proportion of the church of God. "The common people heard him gladly," seems an apt comment on the plain narratives related here. Countless Christian workers would have considered it a pinnacle of achievement just to have developed the rapport and communicative ability which Raymond manifested in this type of work. Behind all the activity was a life and ministry of prayer. This came through when people spoke of Raymond and, even a comparatively short ministry in Templemore Hall had gendered some tales which could easily become legendary. In this category was the account of Raymond going round the seats one evening in Templemore Hall and getting on his knees before each one and praying for the souls who would occupy these at the week-end.

The influence that Jimmy Carson and Tommy Campbell, the expatriate Irishman in Glasgow, exerted upon Raymond in the realm of prevailing prayer in the work of God was considerable. These men poured fuel upon the already existent prayer desire and helped produce the basis for the dynamism which Raymond displayed in all his labours. Harry Gilpin had an interesting anecdote about Jimmy Carson, which probably motivated Raymond's desire to reach formerly "forbidden" Roman Catholic and I.R.A. supporters' areas, like the Short Strand.

Harry recounted the story in this way: "In the midst of the 'Troubles,' God spoke to Jimmy Carson and told him to go and take the Gospel to Unity Flats at the bottom of the Shankill Road. Now Unity Flats are the wildest and strongest Provisional I.R.A. den in the city of Belfast. It is a grim and forbidding, political graffiti-covered eyesore which no ordinary citizen would want to go near. Jimmy said: 'The Lord told me to go there, so off I went with a packet of Gospel tracts.' At the entrance into the flats there is kind of courtyard or square and Jimmy had just reached this when three very rough looking men came out to face him. 'Who are you?' they demanded menacingly, 'Jimmy Carson' he said, 'And I'm a Christian and the Lord has told me to bring the Gospel here.' The middle one of the three men pulled a revolver out of his inside pocket and repeated with an oath, 'You're not coming in here,' and, at the same time, he pulled the trigger as he held the gun aloft and a live bullet exploded out of the muzzle. 'Now do you understand?' the thug said, 'You're not coming in here!' Jimmy looked at him with quiet determination and said: 'You can pull that trigger if you like, but you'll only send me home to my Lord quicker than I anticipated, so if He wants me home right now that's fine by me, but I'm going to carry out His command.' The I.R.A. man fired another shot in the air, but Jimmy remained unmoved and stood his ground. The thug dropped his arm to his side and spat out, 'to hell with this!' and threw the revolver on to the ground and turned away.

Jimmy entered the flats and distributed all his tracts without further interference. There is good evidence uncovered later by Jimmy Carson to support the fact that the unwilling I.R.A. man opted out of the organisation and was eventually found murdered by 'persons unknown'."

A common denominator which motivated Raymond McKeown and Jimmy Carson was a "Valiant-for-Truth" element which permeated their lives and ministry throughout their pilgrimage. Jimmy died a few years later, typically on his knees in the attitude of prayer. This was the posture which poignantly reflected his attitude and response to divine soverignty. Bunyan surely wrote of such pilgrims when he penned his verse of a hymn:

> Who would true valour see,
> Let him come hither;
> One here will constant be,
> Come wind, come weather.

> There's no discouragement,
> Shall make him once relent,
> His first avow'd intent,
> To be a Pilgrim.

Although Belfast could rightly claim the distinction of being the most evangelically minded city in the United Kingdom, it was not spared the ravages of the contemporary permissive society. Raymond was grieved to find the elements of moral filth and pollution spouting like evil spores in the fabric of society in Belfast as they had in Glasgow.

Sex shops appeared in Castlereagh Road, Gresham Street and Belfast city centre. Raymond's actions in objecting to these establishments and their sale of obscene publications, resulted in the seizing of magazines, tapes and films by the Royal Ulster Constabulary in June, 1984. A continual stream of correspondence with various Members of Parliament, the Home Office and the Royal Ulster Constabulary, coupled to direct action in the form of protest marches and open air meetings were organised by Raymond. The outrageous ordeal which he had endured in Glasgow when he and other campaigners against the opening of a "Private Shop" in Partick had been subjected to incessant phone calls from sexual perverts and deviants, had not diminished his resolve to purge the muck wherever it appeared in his vicinity. "The humblest citizen of the land, when clad in the armour of a righteous cause, is stronger than all the hosts of error.*

*Wm. Jennings Bryan. Oxford Dictionary of Quotations.

Chapter 12

Finished The Course

Mrs. Jonathan Edwards, writing from Northampton, Mass., to her brother in 1740, concerning the visit of George Whitefield, said, "He is a truly remarkable man, and during his visit, has, I think, verified all we have heard of him. He makes less of the doctrines than American preachers generally do and aims more at affecting the heart. He is a born orator."*

This assessment could accurately be made of Raymond McKeown also. Strongly rooted in the doctrines of grace and having read copiously in the literature of the Puritans and Scottish Divines of that period, yet many of this Christian acquaintances were unaware of his theological perspectives of which he confessed privately, "I grow more convinced of these truths with every passing year." This lack of aggressive public affirmation of these doctrines was seen as a vice by some, and as a virtue by others. The Isle of Lewis, a stronghold of Calvinistic belief, is, also, perhaps paradoxically in the estimation of some, still the place with the most consistent record of God given revival in all of Europe. Facts like these coupled to Raymond's cheerful, outgoing, happy-go-lucky disposition, his single-minded evangelical fervour, his extempore preaching, love of simple hymns and choruses surely lay an axe to the stereotyped image of the dour, joyless Scottish Calvinist, so often portrayed as devoid of any vestige of true joy and spirituality.

Like so many of God's gifted servants, Raymond seemed to have unlimited time at his disposal. It is a matter beyond dispute that each of us have as much time as anyone else in the world. Some men may have greater gifts, wealth, influence or ability, but we each have twenty four hours in a day. The solemn thing about time is, of course, that it can be lost and time lost can never be regained. It cannot be hoarded; it must be spent. It cannot be postponed; it is irretrievably

---

George Whitefield. Dallimore. Banner of Truth.

lost. How supremely important then, that we make full use of the time allotted to us for the fulfilment of our life purpose. The following quotation engraved on a sundial expresses this truth:

> The shadow by my finger cast
> Divides the future from the past;
> Before it stands the unborn hour
> In darkness and beyond thy power.
> Behind its unreturning line
> The vanished hour, no longer thine,
> One hour alone is in thine hands,
> The NOW on which the shadow stands.

Dr. J. H. Jowett wrote, "I confess as a minister, that the men to whom I most hopefully look for additional service are the busiest men."* Raymond had long realised the significance of this truth. Careless or disorganised in some aspects of life, he may have appeared to be, but he demonstrated a remarkable capacity for cramming more into a day than most men. He seemed to have an innate ability to recognise the things which were of first importance and relegated others so that he never seemed to be trivially employed. It was no imposition upon him to be continually in the service of the Gospel, for this was all his passion in life.

It was Wednesday, 8th May, 1985, and it was Violet's birthday. Raymond had suggested a visit to a Chinese restaurant for a meal to celebrate and thus the birthday gave them the excuse to have a relaxing time out together, which was not a common experience in the busy lifestyle in which they were both engaged. Violet was specially looking forward to the time in view of the hectic unremitting programme which engulfed Raymond in the ministry at Templemore Hall and in Northern Ireland generally. They drove down to University Drive for what was to be their last outing together and settled into a table by a window overlooking the street. Nearing the completion of what proved to be a very enjoyable meal, Raymond suddenly said, "Look at that poor young fellow, Violet." She looked through the window and saw a very inebriated young man with a whisky bottle in one hand, making unsteady progress along the pavement, as he sought to render a favourite ditty to all and sundry.

When they had paid their bill, Violet anticipated a leisurely stroll,

---

*Problems of Christian Discipleship. O. Sanders. O.M.F. Publications.

some window shopping and eventually a return home with the feeling of well being and satisfaction at having one day of unusual relaxation in the midst of the maelstrom of activity which constituted their normal existence. They had not proceeded far when they espied the intoxicated young man sitting somewhat disconsolately in a doorway. Violet's anticipation of spending the rest of the time with Raymond without diversion was soon shattered. As they walked past the doorway she was suddenly conscious that she was talking to herself, for Raymond had disappeared. Looking back, she saw that he had joined the unfortunate drunk in the doorway and was sitting with his arm round his shoulder, speaking quietly, but earnestly. The young fellow, Jerry by name, who was listening intently and with an incredulous look on his face, because, as he expressed it himself, "I cannot believe anybody could be interested in a drunk like me." His appreciation was manifested in the way which doubtless seemed most fitting to him when he offered Raymond a swig from the depleted whisky bottle. After Raymond had kindly informed him that he had drunk from a fountain which far surpassed the liquor in Jerry's hand, he admonished him gently concerning his need of Christ as Saviour. With a little word of prayer, Raymond was on his way. Violet said later, "Wasn't it good that the Lord made our last outing together to include a witness to a needy soul?" Surely Raymond could say with the Psalmist: "Thou shalt guide me with thy counsel, and afterward receive me to glory." Ps. 73:24.

Violet had decided to go over to Scotland around the 13th May, 1985, to visit her father and Judith and Alistair and family. John Jordan had a day off work on Friday, 17th. That morning he said to his wife Marie, "Let's go down to the city centre for some shopping." Marie replied, "Maybe we could go down past the Hall and we can see Raymond there and remind him that he is due to come to us for his meals on Sunday." John and Marie drove from their home in King's Drive, Knock, on to the city ring road and then down Newtownards Road, turning into Templemore Avenue. Arriving at the Hall, John and Marie were greatly surprised to find a small group of Raymond's faithful open air workers huddled together anxiously discussing why Raymond had not appeared for their weekly Friday open air meeting. Having commenced this work it was his pride and joy, so his non appearance was very puzzling.

It was now over an hour past the time for commencement of the open air work and John and Marie joined in the speculative discussion as they all came to the conclusion that, as Raymond had been complaining of a painful back, this was the likely explanation of his absence. Someone mentioned that Raymond had been visiting a relative of one of the church members on Thursday morning, but had not turned up for the mixed choir practice, which was also unusual because he always came along to that gathering. The group eventually broke up to go their several ways.

John and Marie chatted with some of the folks, and then, waving them goodbye, returned to their car and after a moment's discussion decided that they would call at the manse on the way home, in case Raymond was unable to go shopping because of his injured back. As they approached the manse in Orby Drive, John noticed that Raymond's little Toyota Starlet car was sitting in the drive next to the house. John felt a sudden stab of fear and apprehension, mingled with a sense of reproach that he was over reacting a little to a situation which probably had a perfectly reasonable explanation. John was seeking to restrain himself from communicating the increasing unease he was feeling to Marie, when they arrived at the front door and saw the milk bottles there on the door step, still uncollected. There was no disguising the anxiety which this sight promoted in John and Marie as they rang the doorbell repeatedly, but there was no reply.

"Let's get round to the back door quickly," John said, and they hurried round to the rear of the house and stopped to look through the living room window. A light was switched on and Ruth, the black labrador dog, was sitting on the settee. While John was still trying to absorb the implications of all these factors, Marie broke off and ran to the adjacent kitchen window. John heard her shout, "Come quickly. He's lying on the kitchen floor." Because the back door was locked, John smashed a glass panel so that he could gain access. Raymond lay on his back beside the kitchen sink, his glasses beside his outstretched hand. John had the heartbreaking experience of examining him for any sign of life, but it was obvious that he had been dead for some time.

The McKeowns had trained Ruth the dog to bring a cushion in its mouth to any visitors who came to the house. The Jordans noticed that the dog had displayed this affectionate little gesture by surrounding Raymond with cushions as he lay there. A little note which Raymond had been writing, in humorous vein, to his next door neighbour, informing her that Violet was off to Scotland for the week and that she had been having some success with the diet she had been on, contained the last known words of Raymond's this side of eternity. They somehow epitomise that cheery, effervescent, good-natured aspect of his character which so captivated those who knew him.

> O Mrs. Gamble would you please
> take charge of these collected keys,
> For Violet and 'tis no surprise —
> has made her way to "paradise."
> (She is so thin that she got there
> by boat and train for just half fare).
> If you don't have these keys no doubt,
> I'll soon find out that I get locked out
> And if I do I'll have to plan
> to spend the night in the "Sally Ann" . . .

The poem lay half completed, the pen on a table beside the chair where he had laid it as he made his way to the kitchen, perhaps for a glass of water or some medication to ease the pain or distress that probably came upon him.

In a somewhat dazed and grief stricken state, John and Marie contacted some of the office bearers of Templemore Hall, who immediately got in touch with Foster Wright, an expatriate Irish pastor living in Denny, which is just a few miles from Falkirk, where Violet was visiting her family. So the tragic news was broken to her.

The sad tidings soon spread throughout the Christian community and tears were shed in many quiet places when the unbelievable report reached the multitude of fellow saints and friends. They found as Shakespeare said, "Well, every one can master a grief but he that has it."* Raymond was an institution. It was unthinkable that he had gone from this scene of time. At 60 years of age, people just expected that he would be around for a number of years to come. To many folks Raymond had been "a nail in a sure place," "unchanging, immoveable, always abounding in the work of the Lord." He had epitomised the joyful attractive qualities of the Gospel. Ever an unflinching crusader in the warfare against evil, and untiring in his efforts to help and encourage his fellow men. His middle name was Joseph, and like his namesake, he was in his own way "A fruitful bough, even a fruitful bough by a well; whose

---

The Oxford Dictionary of Quotations.

branches run over the wall." Gen. 49:22.

Templemore Hall was crowded to capacity with around 500 mourners gathered to pay their last respects to Raymond McKeown. It is a matter of some bewilderment to those who have no true Christian experience that a spirit of buoyancy and joy can permeate a funeral service where it is also evident that a great loss has been suffered. A huge congregation sung a hymn of revival with its note of expectancy and petition, it expressed the essential spirit of Raymond McKeown. Those who knew him, knew that he would have approved of such an epitaph, because the yearning for a God-given revival was never far from his thoughts or utterance.

When the congregation finally spilled out on to Templemore Avenue in front of the hall, they immediately swelled the hundreds who waited outside, until around a thousand people must have been assembled there. Another hymn was sung by the people in the open air and then four young men, including Raymond's son Paul, carried the coffin on their shoulders down Templemore Avenue for a few hundred yards to the waiting hearse. The massive crowd followed in procession as is the custom in the Province. Normally they would have gone to the cemetery, but, as Raymond was to go home to Scotland to be buried in Falkirk, the mourners proceeded only to the funeral parlour, where many of them returned then to Templemore Hall for some light refreshment before dispersing.

Two days later, on Thursday, 23rd May, 1985, Raymond was interred in the cemetery in Falkirk. It was a miserable, cold, damp and at times torrentially rainy day. An old Scots word describes it perfectly — it was a "dreich" day! The lengthy cortege held up traffic for a considerable time as the crowd wended their sorrowful way to the graveside. Some hundreds attended in spite of the atrocious weather conditions, and several speakers, including ministers and fellow workers, paid tribute, while leaden skies poured unceasing rain upon the mourners with melancholy vengeance. Had Raymond been able to observe the event, it is not irreverent to suggest that he might have indulged in wry smile at the prolix nature of the proceedings in such adverse conditions. Several memorial services, both in Belfast and Glasgow, were held to pay tribute to a man whose attitude to life was summed up in the verse of a hymn sung at his funeral service:

> When all my labours and trials are o'er,
> And I am safe on that beautiful shore,

Just to be near the dear Lord I adore,
Will thro' the ages be glory for me.

Raymond would have strenuously abhorred the possibility of being the subject of any eulogy. It was his God and Saviour who had made him what he was in electing grace. An earlier statement of Willie Docherty, Raymond's co-worker in the Open Air Mission days is worth repeating. "Raymond was a great man, but it was a Great God who made him so." The many people who may have come close to idolising him at times, were basically good Christian people who were certainly not intentionally guilty of this practice. Rather, they were consciously or unconsciously greatly attracted to one in whom the spirit of God had wrought a significant work of grace. Time and history should declare that it was not an evanescent work, precisely because God Himself had sovereignly decreed that in this chosen vessel He had ordained a "master craftsman" for His own purposes, who was always found, "believing where he could not prove."*

Behold a man raised up by Christ!
The rest remaineth unreveal'd,
He told it not; or something seal'd,
The lips of that Evangelist.*

---

*In Memoriam. Tennyson.